Nkrumah's Conscie[nism]
An Ideology for
Decolonization
And Development

Charles Adom Boateng
Kean College of New Jersey

KENDALL/HUNT PUBLISHING COMPANY
4050 Westmark Drive   Dubuque, Iowa 52002

This edition has been printed directly from camera-ready copy.

Copyright © 1995 by Charles Boateng

ISBN 0-7872-1396-9

Printed in the United States of America
10 9 8 7 6

Table of Contents

List of Tables and Illustrations

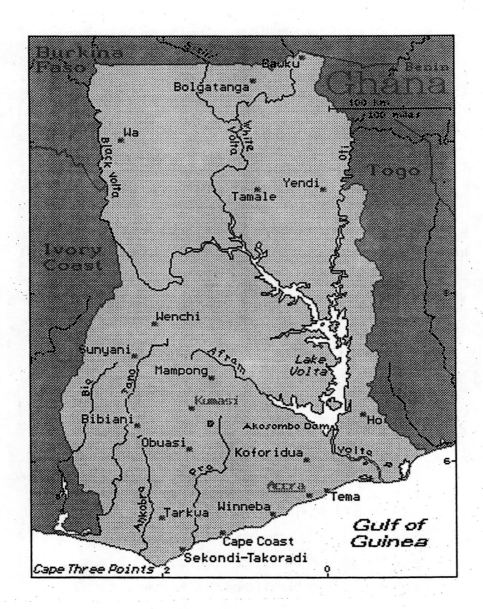

Preface

This study focuses on Nkrumah's perception of the problems third-world countries face in their pursuit of development. Nkrumah's solutions included minimizing the impact of neocolonialism and adopting socialist strategy for development. As president of the first black African country to be independent, Kwame Nkrumah is an elder statesman of the African continent whose ideas on Ghanaian and African development have provided some theoretical and practical understanding of third-world development.

Nkrumah's views on neocolonialism and dependency attempt to explain how the global economy affects Africa's underdevelopment. For third-world countries to develop, Nkrumah believed that the first order of business is to achieve political independence. All the same, he warned developing countries to be wary of possible attempts by developed countries to control their economic sphere even after political independence. He suggested that poor countries should delink from the world capitalist system to avoid neocolonialism.

To tackle the problem of underdevelopment, Nkrumah suggested the socialist model with the state playing a dominant role. Nkrumah's socialism rejects capitalism as a necessary stage towards socialism. Focusing on traditional African communalism to buttress his argument, Nkrumah believed that it was possible to achieve economic abundance without going through capitalism, a notion which was out of line with traditional Marxist thinking.

For a meaningful development, Nkrumah suggested that development of Africa should be carried out on a Pan-African basis. But because emerging countries naturally have problems such as lack of economic resources, Nkrumah had to depend on the East and West for help, a situation which contradicted his policy of self-reliance. Bribery and corruption were not eliminated. Nkrumah was blamed for leading Ghana to the verge of total bankruptcy. His charisma eroded. He became unpopular in Ghana making the success of the military takeover almost inevitable.

In spite of the misgivings about Nkrumah's record he is still remembered as a unique Ghanaian statesman for his modernization programs and the gaining of international recognition for Ghana and Africa.

Special thanks is extended to J. Leo Cefkin, Stephen Mumme, Gilbert White and Charles Kelly for their time, expertise, encouragement and congeniality which made all the difference in completing the research.

I am indebted to Melinda, my loving wife, as well as my children, Carlos, Daniel and Vera, for their incredible support and understanding.

A note of appreciation is also extended to Jeanne Gannon for her patience and reliability in the design, layout and copyediting of this book.

Finally, I wish to thank Opanin D.K. Adom, my uncle, and Maame Yaa Nsiah, my mother, who offered me support, encouragement and academic opportunity.

Charles Adom Boateng
Department of Political Science
Kean College of New Jersey
Union, New Jersey 07083

Chapter 1
Introduction

A major concern of third-world leaders is development of their country after political independence. But despite the agreement on the need for development, major questions about the concept of development do arise. Firstly, what is it that needs to be developed? Secondly, what should be the proper sequence of development? And, thirdly, what should be the means of achieving development? It may be useful in this Introduction to attempt preliminary answers to these three questions about the concept of development.

First: Just what is it that should be developed? There is little clarity about the subjects and objects of development. To the extent that any scholarly agreement can be discerned, it is confined to the importance of the economy, partly, perhaps, because this can apparently be quantified and therefore measured most easily.

Second: What should be the proper sequence of development? The easier accessibility of economic data has led many scholars, and probably, more policy-makers to jump to the conclusion that economic development occurs before development in the other spheres and must be the cause, or at least a precondition, of non-economic development. Now, even if economic development can be segregated, for purely analytical purposes, from development in the social, cultural, and political spheres, the reverse sequence of events seems to be closer to the truth; that is, political development takes place before economic, social and cultural development, and that development of politics can be looked upon as a condition of other, more substantive types of development.[1]

It is from this comparative standpoint that I analyze Dr. Kwame Nkrumah, president of the first black African country to gain political independence. And, like Nkrumah, other black African leaders have generally placed stronger emphasis upon political than upon economic development, and that many of them have professed a belief in and a commitment to the primacy of politics. Specifically, Nkrumah made it clear that without political independence, plans for social and economic revolution will invariably fail. He said, "Seek ye first the political kingdom and all other things will be added unto it." The question then becomes: Does political independence necessarily guarantee economic and social progress? Attempts will be made to answer this question throughout this research.

Third: What should be the means to achieve economic and social progress? Unlike other African leaders, Nkrumah believed that scientific socialism should be the route to follow. There are as many varieties of socialism in Africa as there are independent states to proclaim them. But to Nkrumah, other African states had lost sight of what socialism is supposed to be: "the public ownership of the means of production...to bring benefit to the people."[2]   For socialism to be true to its purpose and not alienated from the people, according to Nkrumah, it must recognize the dialectic and the creativity of the struggle. Scientific socialism must also embrace materialism and translate this into the social terms of equality.[3]

It is worth noting that well-intentioned third-world leaders and men of great vision, who have applied in various degrees the socialist ideology, have come to the same results of near economic collapse and political instability. The almost similar pattern of failure for the newly independent African countries suggests that we should trace the causes to the common problematics of the main development strategy which they applied, socialism itself, be it scientific socialism or African socialism.

The Importance of Nkrumah

Nkrumah is important for a number of reasons:

Third-world leaders are inadequately appreciated as political theorists even though their views have been influential in shaping the future of their countries. As a consequence, there is residue of benign neglect of African political theorists, and scholars do not appreciate their contributions. But for better or for worse, Nkrumah is a figure to reckon with. As president of the first West African country to gain political independence after the Second World War, Nkrumah might well be considered an elder statesman of tropical Africa. His views and theoretical foundations on which they are based contribute, in some degree, to the formation of ideas and actions of both the leaders and the led of the African continent.

Nkrumah left an enduring legacy. He is considered a leading figure in decolonization. In Africa's struggle to liquidate colonialism in all its forms, Nkrumah is both an architect and engineer. He led the Ghanaian anti-colonial nationalism which brought about political independence. All the same, Nkrumah was skeptical about true independence and as a result wrote extensively on neocolonialism which is a condition where a country may be politically independent and still be economically dependent on other states.

Furthermore, Nkrumah was a leading figure in nation-building and state-building. While nation-building concerns the creation of a homogeneous, consensual, and integrated society, state-building involves the establishment of an effective political system to govern the nation. Specifically, Nkrumah stressed the essence of unity among Ghanaians and also among Africans. He detribalized Ghana by denying political power to the various ethnic leaders. He advocated that one was a Ghanaian first before being an Ashanti, Ewe, Fanti, Ga, or Nzimah. Without question, Nkrumah pursued one-party parliamentary system of government which has also been emulated by many African countries.

Moreover, Nkrumah was a leading personality of Pan-Africanism. His Pan-Africanist creed stressed the fact that development can be more effectively applied to Africa only by emphasizing first political unification of African countries. Utilizing the twin examples of the United States and the Soviet Union to prop up his argument for unity, Nkrumah uncompromisingly championed political union rather than the more cautious functional, economic cooperation advocated by the majority of Africa's leaders. Nkrumah's rationale was that if Africa is balkanized, it will be at the mercy of colonialism and imperialism. Even though Nkrumah's idea of an African federation did not succeed, the formation of the Organization of African Unity (OAU) was a significant achievement.

A major theoretical contribution of Nkrumah is evident in his notion "consciencism." The major dimensions of Nkrumah's philosophical consciencism are: a) that independence should be won by the people for the people; b) that socialism should be the means towards development; c) that socialism should not be alienated from the people. Thus, socialism should seek a connection with the equalitarian and the humanist past of the people before their social evolution was ravaged by colonialism; d) that foreign and private interests should not dominate society; and e) that the state should defend the independence and security of the people.[4]

Thus, consciencism presupposes that the only way to achieve development is for poor countries to become independent, and after that to delink from the world capitalist system and avoid neocolonialism. Also, it suggests that the preferred path towards development is to adopt socialism with the state playing a dominant role.

Nkrumah was a great initiator of African debates. This does not mean that Africans agreed with him. Moreover, he provoked much enthusiasm in Africa and predictable contempt abroad. He was both creator and victim of transition from pre-modern to modern industrial society.

Nkrumah provides a very good example of a leader who disseminates Western and Eastern political ideas to their people and other leaders. Nkrumah's political ideas were stimulated by Marx, Lenin, Garvey, Padmore, Gandhi and also his own African traditional background. Just as we cannot dismiss the foreign influence, neither can we ignore those ideas which originate from their traditional outlooks. Nkrumah was educated in the West and became familiar with Western and Eastern political thought. But what is significant is that Nkrumah, like other African political theorists, did not accept these ideas in toto, but attempted to adapt them to suit the African conditions. Thus, Nkrumah was a syncretic theorist (that is, he used Western political thought giving it an African expression).

Theories of Dependency and Modernization

Many scholars have sought to explain why African countries remain underdeveloped. Those scholars tend to focus on two broad competing paradigms or models of theoretical understanding that seek to explain why some countries are poor and others are wealthy. These are the theory of modernization and the theory of dependency.

Modernization theorists assert that a society is either modern or traditional; that role differentiation is an indicator of modernization; that modernized society can innovate without falling apart; and that industrialization is necessary but not sufficient for modernization.[5] Thus, modernization theories blame underdeveloped society for its lack of societal capacity as responsible for its underdevelopment. Some of these assumptions of modernization theory can be misleading. For instance, modernization theorists view modernity and tradition as polar opposites and conclude that in order

to modernize, the third-world societies must overcome their traditional-
isms. In fact, there is a lack of clean break between pre-modern and modern
societies. The concept of underdevelopment makes sense only as a way of
comparing levels of development.

Dependency theorists, on the other hand, derive their concepts from
Marxist sources. In a nutshell, they argue that the wealth and poverty of
nations result from the global process of exploitation. This is the situation
André Gunder Frank refers to as "the development of underdevelopment."[6] Thus, the problem of the poor countries is not lack of technological knowhow, cultural traits conducive to development, or modern institutions, but that they have been subjected to the exploitation of the international capitalist system and its special imperialist agents, both domestic and
alien. The infiltration of western capital into the poor countries has resulted
in situations characterized by economists as "growth without development," as in the particular cases of Ivory Coast and Liberia.

The concept of "dependency" coined by Brazilian sociologist
Fernando Henriqué Cardoso, helps to link both economic and political
analysis; that is, it links those who are the beneficiaries of development with
those who make the decisions. Dependency simply states that crucial economic decisions are made not by the countries that are being "developed"
but by foreigners whose interests are carefully safeguarded. And that foreigners use their economic power to buy political power in the countries
that they penetrate. The collusion between alien economic and political
power distorts both the economy and the policy of the dependent countries. Out of this situation emerged political alliances between domestic and
foreign bourgeoisie. The process is now complete because just as the
metropoles exploits the colonies, so does the domestic colonial bourgeois
class exploit the rest of the population.[7] Thus, before African countries can
develop, there must be a profound analysis of Africa's position in the global
economy and the international stratification of power, as well as an appreciation of the growing complexity of Africa's class structure.

In short, while modernization theorists blame lack of societal capacity as
responsible for Africa's underdevelopment, dependency theorists blame
mostly external hegemonic forces, and, to a lesser extent, internal bourgeoisie as contributing to Africa's underdevelopment. It must be noted that
both modernization and dependency theorists do an adequate job explain-
ing underdevelopment in Africa. However, they both fail to address scien-

tific socialism, the understanding of which is necessary for the understanding of Nkrumah's political thought. While Nkrumah's socialism addresses the rejection of capitalism (anti-colonialism), and the need to reflect African traditional structures, modernization theorists call on the third-world countries to emulate the processes and institutions that western societies used to achieve their development. Moreover, modernization theory assumes that if a country wants to develop, it must also do away with its traditional society and culture. This notion is contrary to Nkrumah's socialism which advocates the institutionalization of the African traditional structures. Thus, unlike the modernization theorists, Nkrumah believed that modernity and tradition can coexist.

The dependency theory, on the other hand, which employs the theory of imperialism has as its key concepts terms such as "neocolonialism," "anti-imperialism," and "exploitation." These were ideas Nkrumah took on nearly a decade before the dependency perspective became popular. Both Nkrumah and the dependency school blame, in the most part, external hegemonic forces as responsible for third-world's underdevelopment. They also recognize the possible alliance between domestic and foreign bourgeoisie. Looking at these similarities, it can be said that the dependency school rather than the modernization theories better illustrates and thus helps us to better understand Nkrumah's notion of Africa's development and underdevelopment.

To correct the distortions and obstacles of development caused by dependency, a prominent Soviet scholar, Ivan Potekhin, has suggested the socialist model. While Potekhin posits that socialism is a universal, rigid concept,[8] Nkrumah disagrees on the grounds that socialism can yield the expected outcome only if it is pragmatically applied to suit the African condition. As a consequence, Nkrumah and Potekhin have fundamental differences regarding the class question. In this connection, Nkrumah is a Marxist but a unique one who syncretically adapts Marxism to Ghana. In this light, Nkrumah has some distinct ideological distortions which included his conspiratorial theory of politics, particularly his distortion of neocolonialism, his treatment of class competition, and his theory of the centralized role of the state.[9] (A complete discussion of Nkrumah's socialism is discussed in Chapter 2.)

In the chapters to follow, such themes as neocolonialism, class questions, socialism, and the role of foreign capital will be pursued, all of which are ideas shared by Nkrumah and the dependency school. Dependency theory does not address the importance of the individual leader.

Nkrumah's Charismatic Personality

For a better understanding of the implementation and effectiveness of Nkrumah's socialist strategies to develop Ghana, a discussion of Nkrumah's charismatic personality in Ghanaian and African politics is appropriate. A charismatic appeal may be defined as "a certain quality of an individual personality by which he is set apart and treated as endowed with supernatural, superhuman, or at least specifically exceptional powers or qualities."[10] There are a number of attributes or characteristics that some scholars believe are common to charismatic leaders. Some see charismatic leaders as omniscient. The leader is seen as a demi-god.[11] They are looked on as prophets who are believed to possess cognitive vision of the future. Articles of Nkrumaism in the Ghanaian newspapers compared Nkrumah with Jesus and Moses by referring to him as the "liberator, Messiah, Christ of our day."[12] Certain events in Nkrumah's life were described by his followers in terms reminiscent of New Testament accounts of the life of Christ. For instance, from time to time, Nkrumah went for a visit in the western part of Ghana. *The Evening News* newspaper described such retreats as days of "fasting and meditation."[13] Implicit in this description was the similarity between Nkrumah's retreats and Christ's meditation in the desert.

Also, when Nkrumah broke away from the United Gold Coast Convention (UGCC), the first nationalist party as Secretary-General, the members were said to have "turned against him and scorned him."[14] On another occasion, Nkrumah rowed a boat across a river in order to reach a village during a tour through Ghana. The comparison was made between this event and Christ's teaching on the boat in the words:

> The Leader Kwame Nkrumah rowing a boat containing a man over the river Oti to fulfill an appointment is symbolic of the new spirit in Africa.... No doubt on that day when the leader was rowing his followers over the River Oti he must have been asking them to dump into the river the old doubts and fears, telling them to cast away past regrets, hate, vindictiveness, envy and spite, for there is no time for these soul-destroying diseases in the life of any African, the time is short and small states at loggerheads with each other will be easy prey to the mechanization of imperialism.[15]

Ghanaians were not only to read about Nkrumah's association with Christ, they were to perceive and see in him such personality as well. Postcards with certain pictures were printed for sale. One card showed Christ and Nkrumah together.[16] And, another showed Nkrumah being given the key to paradise by Christ.[17] Moreover, his image appeared on Ghana's currency and postage stamps.

Thus, Nkrumah was looked at as almost a mythical person. The leader was also seen as outstanding in wisdom, outstanding in prescience and possessing the power to bring into reality the goals the Ghanaians share. Some people feel that a charismatic leader has a supernatural gift of healing. Indians attributed their recovery from illness to touching Gandhi's apparel or repeatedly chanting Gandhi's name. Others also believe that charismatic leaders have a high energy level and are able to maintain late hours. And, also they are not easily frightened, disconcerted or thrown off balance. They possess coolness and humor in the face of danger or crisis. Charismatic leaders are believed to possess excellent memory. Another stereotype some attribute to charismatic leaders is that they are exposed to a wide variety of social environments. This makes them able to appeal to a wider group of people. Some have suggested that charismatic leaders usually emerge under stress or by a revolution. There also exists the myth of invulnerability. Others think that leaders who command charismatic appeal are responsive to dominant values and tradition.

Physically, some people feel that charismatic leaders have extraordinary eyes which they describe as long and charming. Also the leader is seen as one who resists neocolonism and imperialism. Emphasis is put on their extraordinary use of allusions, metaphors, similes, rhythm, repetition, and alliteration. Scholars also agree that the maintenance of the charismatic relationship depends on the continued ability to provide results.[18] In discussing the decline of charismatic authority, James V. Downton stresses that when leaders fail to show results, there is a decline in popularity which renders them incapable to coerce, thereby reducing followers' commitment.[19]

The basis of Nkrumah's personality projection was a somewhat vague philosophical notion referred to as Nkrumaism. Although Nkrumaism and the later philosophy consciencism were not taught on a formal basis until after 1960, Nkrumaism had been introduced before the founding of the Republic in 1960. Kofi Baako, one of Nkrumah's advisors, was its leading exponent.[20] Nkrumaism was promoted by the League of Ghana Patriots, the National Association of Socialist Students' Organization (NASSO), and the Convention Peoples Party Vanguard Activists.[21]

There was no agreed-upon definition of what Nkrumaism entails. But, generally, the term was used in reference to Nkrumah's political concepts in the development of an African philosophy that could be political, cultural, religious, moral, economic or social in nature. But that the proponents of Nkrumaism became so lost in their own jargon, that little, if any, meaningful philosophy of African development was created. An examination of a number of definitions of Nkrumaism suggests how meaningless and contradictory the term became. In the *Evening News*, the religious dimension of Nkrumaism was emphasized:

> *Nkrumaism is ... the highest form of christianity, etc., in an age of greed and hypocrisy which teaches that you must remove all these root causes of hate and jealousy among haves and have-nots in order to make it humanly possible to love one's neighbor as one's self in a more enduring way.*[22]

Two months later, another thought appeared: "Nkrumaism is a constructive alternative, a direct and positive challenge to the hypocrisy underlying the civilization we have known for two thousand years of Christendom."[23] The political dimension of Nkrumaism was alluded to in the following: "Nkrumaism is ... based on the common people's inevitable rise from the scum of the earth to take their place in the sun, a theory springing from a people with a long tradition of collectivization and faith in majority rule and Democratic Centralism."[24] Political thought and economics were combined in another editorial in the *Evening News:* "The originality underlying Nkrumaism is particularly marked in the Economic Theory, which, as may have been noted ... is indissolubly linked with the Political Philosophy."[25] Also, the social implications of Nkrumaism were explained in terms of a "theory of crisis of human relations."[26] Nkrumaism, then, was based on a number of Nkrumah's ideas, put together to form a vague, unsystematized philosophy.

As part of the Nkrumaism, Nkrumah's Marxist influence was suggested in political, economic, and social aspects. This included socialism, democratic centralism, and economic determinism. What the proponents of Nkrumaism did not do was to discuss how these facets would occur historically. It could also be speculated that the religious dimension of

Nkrumaism may have been intended as a replacement of christianity in Ghana. After all, Nkrumah was regarded as a demi-god, and if Nkrumah was a demi-god, then Nkrumaism was the embodiment of his teachings.

From the above discussions, one could deduce that Nkrumah was portrayed in such roles as leader and as a demi-god. Concentrating on the leadership aspect, it is reasonable to assert that Nkrumaism was to be Africa's philosophical response to the Western and Eastern philosophies. Nkrumah was also regarded as an all-conquering warrior (Osagyefo), spiritual director and teacher and it was Nkrumaism that made the Ghanaians to perceive him in all these symbolic roles. And, Nkrumah also employed external rhetorical strategies in attempting to fulfill this task which contributed to his rhetorical personality and his overall personality cult–charisma.

Plan for the Study

In this research, I will rely on available archival and recorded sources. The information obtained from these sources will be carefully analyzed keeping in mind the objective of presenting Nkrumah's development ideology and how that affects Ghana and Africa generally.

The research is divided into seven chapters. An overview of the frameworks for understanding Nkrumah's political thought is established in Chapter 2. The first part of the chapter introduces the theoretical frameworks in the comparative tradition against which Nkrumah will be compared. Specifically, the Marxian, Weberian, and the dependency perspectives as they relate to development are presented. The second part is devoted to the analyses of Nkrumah's theoretical understanding of how the global economy affects Ghanaian and African underdevelopment. Among the important themes discussed are Nkrumah's views on neocolonialism and dependency, all of which attempt to explain how external hegemonic forces affect underdevelopment. The third section of the chapter addresses Nkrumah's views related to the national political responses to the development problem. This section begins with an analysis of Nkrumah's notion of the necessity of political independence, then a discussion of his view of the state and the class question, how the party should be organized, his socialism, and finally, his view of Pan-Africanism as an instrument for fomenting Ghanaian and African development. Chapter 2 concludes with a summary of Nkrumah's political philosophy and its basic policy implications.

Chapter 3 focuses on the factors shaping the political and economic conditions of the Gold Coast (prior to Nkrumah). A review of the Ghanaian colonial past will be pursued emphasizing the Indirect Rule system as well as the economic and social conditions. This will concentrate on the political, economic and social legacy Nkrumah inherited. Also, there will be a brief discussion of the life and career of Nkrumah stressing his political activities both in the U.S. and Britain, his return to the Gold Coast, and his rise to power.

Analyses of programs Nkrumah embarked upon are presented in Chapter 4. Specifically, this chapter illustrates how Nkrumah implemented his socialism, emphasizing his industrialization program, and his social policies such as education, health, and agriculture. Also, this chapter discusses Nkrumah's relationship with traditional authorities, the nature of his bureaucracy, and, finally a discussion of how he tried to use his one-party system and Pan-Africanism to bolster his socialist orientation.

Chapter 5 presents a discussion of the Volta River Project (VRP), the largest industrialization scheme Nkrumah embarked on. For his industrialization program to work, Nkrumah embarked on the building of the VRP to provide power for the industries in Ghana and also to provide power to other neighboring African countries. Even though the Volta Dam provided hydroelectric power for industry and agriculture, improved fisheries, employment, and lake transportation, it cost Ghana too much money to build the VRP. Moreover, the VRP created resettlement and health problems. Others have also criticized Nkrumah for his decision to undertake such a big venture. But, on balance, the decision to build the VRP was a viable one as Ghanaians today still consider the VRP as Nkrumah's most important industrial legacy.

Chapter 6 is devoted to the discussion of the problems Nkrumah faced which eventually led to his decline. Nkrumah was blamed for his massive industrialization program which brought Ghana to the brink of total bankruptcy. His regime was also accused as being corrupt. Some accused him of being a dictator who controlled Ghana. Moreover, others were unhappy about the progress he made and quickly accused Nkrumah for devoting too much time to Pan-African affairs instead of Ghanaian problems. He promised a lot, but relative to his promises, accomplished little and thus shattered the high expectations of the Ghanaians. Consequently, he was overthrown on February 24, 1966, by the military.

The last chapter will present the summary and conclusions of the study. An attempt will be made to recapitulate and discuss the contributions and legacy of Nkrumah as a political theorist and as a policy-maker and government practitioner. Also, a critical appraisal of Nkrumah's rule, especially his pursuit of development and the outcome of his development motive will be carefully discussed. Finally, the chapter will conclude with an overall summary appraisal of Nkrumah's significance generally, and for Africa in particular.

Endnotes

[1] Herbert J. Spiro, "The Primacy of Political Development," *Africa: The Primacy of Politics,* Herbert J. Spiro, ed. (New York: Random House Inc., 1966), pp. 150-169.

[2] *Building a Socialist State: An Address ... to the C.P.P. Study Group, April 22, 1961* (Accra: Ghana Information Services, 1961), p. 2.

[3] Kwame Nkrumah, *Consciencism: Philosophy and Ideology for Decolonization and Development* (New York: Monthly Review Press, 1965), pp. 105-206

[4] Ibid., pp. 78-106

[5] David E. Apter, *The Politics of Modernization* (Chicago: The University of Chicago Press, 1965), pp. 56; 62-67; 187-188. Also, check John H. Kautsky, *The Political Consequences of Modernization* (New York: John Wiley and Sons, Inc., 1972), pp. 19-22

[6] Ronald H. Chilcote, *Theories of Development and Underdevelopment* (Boulder: Westview Press, 1984), pp. 86-96.

[7] Fernando Henriqué Cardoso, *Dependency and Development.* Translated by Marjory Mattingly Urquidi (Berkeley: University of California Press, 1979), p. xvi.

[8] Ivan I. Potekhin, "On African Socialism: A Soviet View," in William H. Friedland and Carl G. Rosberg (eds.). *African Socialism* (Stanford: Stanford University Press, 1964), pp. 97-112.

[9] Kwame Nkrumah, *The Autobiography of Kwame Nkrumah* (New York: Thomas Nelson and Sons, 1957.)

[10]   Ann Ruth Willner, *Charismatic Political Leadership* (Princeton: Princeton University Press, 1960), p. 3; and also Talcott Parsons, "Introduction," in Max Weber (ed.), *The Theory of Social and Economic Organization* (New York: Free Press, 1947), p. 358

[11]   James V. Downton, *Rebel Leadership* (New York: The Free Press, 1973), pp. 209-236

[12]   David Apter, "Ghana," in James S. Coleman and Carl G. Rosberg (eds.), *Political Parties and National Integration in Tropical Africa* (Berkeley: University of California Press, 1964), p. 304; also, Bankhole Timothy, *Kwame Nkrumah: His Rise to Power* (Evanston: Northwestern University Press, 1961), p. 78

[13]   *Evening News,* June 8, 1959, p. 1; also December 11, 1959.

[14]   *Evening News,* September 22, 1958, p. 1.

[15]   *Evening News,* February 4, 1960, p. 2

[16]   D. Warner, *Ghana and the New Africa.* (London: Frederick Muller Press, 1960), p. 93.

[17]   R. Italiaander, *The New Leaders of Africa* (Englewood Cliffs, N.J.; Prentice Hall, 1961), pp. 239-249.

[18]   Downton, *Rebel Leadership,* pp. 209-236; W.G. Runciman, "Charismatic Legitimacy and One-Party Rule in Ghana," *European Journal of Sociology,* 4 (1963), pp. 148-165; and Willner, *Charismatic Political Leadership,* pp.61-103.

[19]   Downton, *Rebel Leadership,* p. 220; also, Robert C. Tucker, "The Theory of Charismatic Leadership," *Daedalus,* 97 (summer 1968), pp. 731-755; Willner, Charismatic Political Leadership, p. 9.

[20]   T.P. Omari, *Kwame Nkrumah: The Anatomy of an African Dictatorship* (Accra: Moxon Paperbacks, 1970), p. 115

[21]   H. Bretton, *The Rise and Fall of Kwame Nkrumah* (London: Pall Mall, 1967), p. 83; also, *The Spark: Some Essential Features of Nkrumaism* (Accra: Spark Publications, 1964).

[22]   *Evening News,* January 26, 1960, p. 2.

[23]   *Evening News,* March 23, 1960, p. 2.

[24]   *Evening News,* November 20, 1959, p. 2

[25]   *Evening News,* March 23, 1960, p. 1.

[26]   *Evening News,* June 22, 1960, p. 2

Discussion Questions

1. Elaborate on the main competing paradigms some scholars have used to explain the causes of the third-world's underdevelopment.

2. Does charisma play a dominant role in political leadership? Explain your answer.

3. Discuss the theoretical contributions of Nkrumah to African political thought.

Chapter 2

Frameworks for Understanding Nkrumah

A wealth of factual and theoretical studies have been produced in the comparative politics literature which attempt to view the problems of underdevelopment broadly and to construct a conceptual framework by which we might better understand what is going on in developing countries. In spite of the distinctive nature of Nkrumah's political thought, recurrent themes exist in his political philosophy that are shared by scholars in the comparative politics tradition. The purpose of this chapter is to lay the foundations for understanding Nkrumah's political philosophy, where it fits in the comparative politics tradition, and what Nkrumah attempted to do for Ghana and Africa.

It is from this standpoint that I propose to first present the theoretical expositions of Marx, Weber, and the dependency school, all of which have contributed to the understanding of the politics of developing areas. The second section of this chapter is devoted to the discussion of Nkrumah's theoretical understanding of how the global economy affects African underdevelopment in general and Ghanaian underdevelopment in particular. Here, we will analyze Nkrumah's views on development and underdevelopment, his concept of neocolonialism, his view on foreign assistance and how these ideas parallel and/or deviate from the dependency line. The third section will address Nkrumah's positions related to the national political responses to the development problem. This section will begin with an analysis of Nkrumah's view of the necessity of political independence; followed by his outlook on the character of the state and class question, party organization, socioeconomic planning, and international affairs (Pan Africanism). The last section will present a summary and conclusion describing the nature of Nkrumah's political philosophy and how these political ideas are implied in his public policies.

Comparative Intellectual Tradition

The major comparative traditions on development which Nkrumah's ideas will be compared to include Marx, Weber, and the dependency perspectives. A summary of their individual political positions will now be presented.

Marx

Karl Marx is one of the early major political thinkers whose ideas have substantially influenced the comparative intellectual tradition by providing the starting point for future investigations. As a precursor of the comparative politics perspective, Marx's ideas on development and also on state and class help us to understand history and social transformation.

In *The Communist Manifesto,* Marx and Engels implied that the state is the instrument of the ruling classes. Specifically, they wrote that the executive of the state "is but a committee for managing the affairs of the whole bourgeoisie." [1] Thus, the capitalist ruling class exercises the power to use the state as its instrument for a domination of society.

The concept of state allowed Marx to focus on bourgeois or capitalist politics; and the concept of class served as the foundation of Marx's understanding of the political economy. In *The Communist Manifesto,* Marx and Engels emphasized that there are two principal classes under capitalism—one that lives by owning; the other by working. [2] Thus, Marx analyzed society in terms of a dominant or ruling class and a working class.

Marx offered an important conception of the state and its ruling class. He believed that all history was the struggle of classes. He argued that under capitalism society will eventually polarize into the bourgeoisie and proletarian classes which will be mutually antagonistic. [3] Marx defines the bourgeoisie class as the owners of the means of production and the class that hold power. The state maintains the property relations of the wealthy minority and therefore supports the oppression of one class by another. The state does not stand above classes but it is always on the side of the rulers. The state, therefore, does not represent all the people, exploiters and exploited. Marx also envisioned the ultimate abrogation of the state and ruling class by the proletariat. [4]

This analysis of state and class is relevant to Nkrumah's concept of the state and class. Even though Nkrumah borrowed from Marx's ideas of the state and classes, in the most part, he diverges from Marx on the question of social classes and the class struggle. Nkrumah's views on the state and class and how they are interrelated to Marx's contention on these matters will be detailed in another section.

It must be noted that another relevance of Marx to Nkrumah is evident in Marx's treatment of the issue of development.

According to Marx, development is a stage. He made this clear in *The Communist Manifesto* by stating that:

> *We see then that the means of production and of exchange, which served as the foundation for the growth of the bourgeoisie, were generated in feudal society. At a certain stage in the development of these means of production and of exchange, the conditions under which feudal society produced and exchanged, the feudal organization of agriculture and manufacturing industry, in a word, the feudal relations of property became no longer compatible with the already developed productive forces; they became so many fetters. They had to be burst asunder; they were burst asunder.* [5]

Thus, development is the capitalist stage of development and beyond. And everything before capitalist stage is underdevelopment. This means that for Marx, development is a stage that is post-feudal. Marx did not write about the third world per se, the concept had not yet emerged.

Moreover, Marx advanced the notion that development does not happen spontaneously; there have to be agents of development. In the feudal era, the bourgeoisie was the agent of social development. The bourgeoisie continued as agent of development through capitalism and beyond. [6] Thus, development beyond capitalism becomes the role of the proletariat. It must also be noted that capitalists do away with things that will enhance further development as further development would imply the increase in productivity. Capitalists would rather produce less and make the same profit than to increase production. In fact, capitalists do establish monopolies which makes it possible to increase their rate of profit without increasing production.

Marx also stated that capitalists do not restrict their activities to one area but try to establish themselves everywhere. He made this point in *The Communist Manifesto*: "The bourgeoisie has through its exploitation of the world market given a cosmopolitan character to production and consumption in every country."[7] Thus, capitalists try to establish themselves in the world market. This notion of the internationalization of capital has been taken on by Lenin. According to Lenin, there comes a stage when capitalism becomes imperialist.[8] (See the next section of this chapter for a complete discussion of Lenin's explanation of how imperialism works.) It must, however, be noted that even though capital is exported to third-world countries, a real dilemma does exist. The dilemma is that third-world countries remain underdeveloped. This is because capitalists do not export enough capital necessary to industrialize the third world.

Thus, contemporary Marxists and Leninists view underdevelopment in the third world as a result of capitalist exploitation of those countries. This notion will be expanded later on as we analyze what Nkrumah has to say about development.

Weber

Unlike Marx, Weber believed that the state can legitimately apply physical force to ensure harmony and order among diverse interests. Weber defined politics as "striving to share power or striving to influence the distribution of power, either among states or among groups within a state." [9] In other words, the state ensures the sanctioning of a plurality of interests.

Weber also believed that in capitalism, the state promotes routinization and efficiency through rational distribution of organizational skills within the bureaucracy. This view of the state allowed Weber to view class in purely economic terms. According to Weber, a class exists "when a) a number of people have in common a specific causal component of their life chances insofar as b) this component is represented exclusively by economic interests in the possession of goods and opportunities for income, and c) is represented under the conditions of the commodity or labor markets." [10]

In summary, Marx and Lenin saw development as a capitalist stage and beyond. They also recognized that capitalists try to establish themselves everywhere. Lenin noted that there comes a stage when capitalism becomes imperialist. While Marx emphasizes inevitable class confrontation and struggle, Weber sees harmony among diverse interests. Also, while Marx stresses ownership and control of the means of production as an explanation of domination and exploitation of one class by another, Weber emphasizes various status groups competing for power. Finally while Marx saw the state on the side of the ruling class, Weber understood the state as the mediating and moderating force that ensures stability and order among all classes and groups.

The Dependency Perspective

In his *Imperialism: The Highest Stage of Capitalism*, Lenin wrote:

> *Not only are there two main groups of countries, those owning countries, and the colonies themselves, but also the diverse forms of dependent countries which, politically, are independent but in fact are enmeshed in the net of financial and diplomatic dependency.*[11]

This quotation clearly indicates Lenin's contributions to a theory of underdevelopment and dependency. Undoubtedly, Lenin's view is an economic interpretation of imperialism. This view of Lenin is now echoed by the concept of "neocolonialism" in Africa and Latin American countries. In Africa, it was Nkrumah who first followed up the Leninist view of neocolonialism; and in Latin America the concept of neocolonialism has been implied in the dependency tradition. (Lenin also wrote about the conflict between national bourgeoisie and the imperialists.)

Nkrumah falls within the mainstream of third-world leaders who were willing to work for a change of their political systems. And, Nkrumah, like the dependency theorists, had ideas on underdevelopment which first became popular after the Second World War. Much of the dependency literature appears after Nkrumah's writing and so he did not draw directly on it to develop his views. Yet Nkrumah parallels the dependency paradigm in many respects and can therefore be looked at as a precursor of the dependency perspective.

Dependency tradition is a neo-Marxist theory which became popular in the 1960s. This theory is used to explain world poverty. According to this perspective, the world is divided into centers and peripheries, with gains from international transactions always in favor of the developed center states.[12]

Several major themes have emerged from the dependency literature and scholars have taken various intellectual positions on those themes. Among the major themes in the theories of dependency which help to explain underdevelopment are: a) the structuralist perspective which focuses on the center-periphery thesis. Its main supporters include Raul Prebisch, Osvado Sunkel, Celso Furtado, Johan Galtung, and André Gunder Frank; b) the "internal colonialism" perspective sees the exploitation as coming from within the country. Pablo Gonzalez Casanova and Fernando Henriqué Cardoso have taken this position; and c) the "new dependency" tradition which asserts that the peripheral economies remain dependent even when they no longer produce raw materials. The main proponents are Fernando Henriqué Cardoso and Enzo Faletto.

The Structuralist Perspective. Prebisch, a Latin American, and eventually the director of the Economic Commission of Latin America (ECLA) formulated the early division of the world into center (industrialized) and periphery (underdeveloped) countries. The ECLA sought for solutions to the negative consequences, that is, the underdevelopment of Latin American countries.[13]

Prebisch's main argument was that the terms of trade were to the advantage of exporters of industrial goods while exporters of agricultural products gained virtually nothing from the trade relationship. He believed, however, that both the center and periphery can benefit if they maximize production, income, and consumption. As a solution to this deterioration of the terms of trade which makes the periphery poorer and dependent, he suggested the industrialization of the periphery and also the need to protect the prices of raw materials of the periphery. Moreover, Prebisch suggested the need for the state to assume a dominant economic role rather than socialize the means of production by coordinating private and public enterprise to overcome the contradictions between the core and the periphery. [14]

Like Prebisch, Sunkel and Furtado shared a structural approach in which capitalist centers were distinguishable from peripheral areas and they tended to analyze underdevelopment by reference to deteriorating terms of trade. Sunkel agreed that accumulation tends to be directed towards special groups. He saw dependency and marginalization as reflections of dependent state capitalism and the activities of foreign investors. To solve the problem of underdevelopment, he suggested several reforms which include: agrarian reform, the need to use agricultural exports to finance industrialization, and the need to reorganize industry away from the wealthy minority. [15] Furtado related the structure of social classes to peripheral capitalism and external dependence. He believed that struggle among classes is usually absent in underdeveloped countries because class consciousness is low. He went on to argue that in Brazil, because of inflation, there was no need for one to identify with the class struggle as employers are more likely to grant wage increases than to oppose strikers because the consumer ultimately pays for the increases.

This condition of peripheral capitalism can be best tackled through the adoption of central planing to promote autonomous capitalism. And to achieve autonomous capitalism, import substitution and industrialization should be pursued. [16] All three, Prebisch, Sunkel, and Furtado analyze the exploitive nature of capital but Sunkel and Furtado emphasize that capitalism cannot reproduce itself in the periphery so as to serve the needs of majority of the people.

Johan Galtung also emphasized the structural theory of imperialism. To Galtung, imperialism is an asymmetrical relationship between more harmonious and richer states on one hand, and less harmonious and poorer states on the other. He believed that the rich exploit the poor nations, impede their economic development, and keep them internally and externally disunited as well. The other side of his argument is that it is the poor countries who have to be blamed since their economic and social cleavages enable rich countries to exploit the poor ones. The biggest problem Galtung saw with poor countries is their production of materials which are in abundant supply. The only way Galtung saw imperialism ending was for the weak and poor countries cooperating and uniting in order to become strong and rich. [17]

André Gunder Frank was influenced by the ECLA structuralist approach. Frank's dichotomy of metropolis and satellite paralleled the ECLA formula of center and periphery. [18] However, Frank was a critic of ECLA, which led him to an anti-capitalist and a Marxist position. As a consequence, he rejected the stage theory of Rostow which advances the argument that development takes place through a succession of stages and that underdevelopment today may pass through higher stages of development. Like other dependency theorists discussed in this section, Frank sees underdevelopment as a consequence of capitalist exploitation.

Internal Colonialism. Casanova and Cardoso used the center-periphery formulation in their own unique views, known as "internal colonialism" and dependent capitalist development, respectively. Unlike other countries which experienced exploitation from the outside, according to Casanova, in Mexico, the exploitation occurs from within. This is what is referred to as internal colonialism. Thus, internal colonialism is the situation where those exploited are being exploited by their own countrymen.

For instance, Indians are exploited and dependent on a dominant society of Spanish Creoles and Latinos. To resolve this problem, Casanova suggested a capitalist approach. He argued that through capitalist development, a bourgeois democracy will evolve, and national integration, stability, and harmony will be achieved. [19] Now, Mexico has a mixed economy of state-guided capitalism. Therefore, the pure capitalist solution Casanova suggested will probably not occur because of the structure of power and the nature of the Mexican revolution.

New Dependency. Focusing on underdevelopment and development, Cardoso and Faletto saw the ECLA paradigm for the analysis of development in Latin America as a compelling one. Like Prebisch, Sunkel, and Furtado, they emphasized that the reason some countries are poor and others rich is because some countries are producers of only raw materials (poor) while others are producers of industrial goods. [20] Their approach is dialectical which emphasizes "not just structural conditioning of social life, but also the historical transformation of structures by conflict, social movements, and class struggles." [21] What makes Cardoso and Faletto different from the other dependency theorists is that the former stress functional and structural dependency that relates external forces (multinational firms, foreign technology, international financial systems, foreign armies working in behalf of imperialism) and internal forces (local dominant classes). Cardoso and Faletto advance the argument that there are two types of dependency: enclave economies in which foreign investment penetrates into local productive processes; and economies controlled by local bourgeoisie. They conclude that an economic system is dependent "when the accumulation and expansion of capital cannot find its essential dynamic component inside the system." [22] Thus, peripheral economies remain dependent even when they no longer produce only raw materials. This is what Cardoso refers to as "new dependency" in which industrialization in the periphery provides products not for mass consumption as in the center but for consumption by the bourgeoisie. [23] Cardoso disagrees with the speculation of Furtado that the national bourgeoisie could contain international capitalism and promote development along autonomous national lines. He believes that Furtado's thesis is no longer relevant because of the new hegemony under the military regime. As a solution to the problem of underdevelopment, Cardoso suggested that the dominant classes must join with international capital with the state as the ultimate authority to implement policies that promote capital expansion. [24]

Criticisms

The dependency theory has several weaknesses. Firstly, there is a lack of unified dependency theory. Secondly, there are only a few studies that have attempted to apply assumptions of dependency to real situations. Thirdly, in setting forth its center-periphery thesis, the ECLA correctly linked under-development to the international system, yet the thesis neglects a close examination of the policies and specific needs of the nations at the center. Finally, dependency theory suffers from weak conceptualization. For instance, Casanova's "internal colonial" model stresses national rather than external conditions. The emphasis on internal conditions may be misleading. The belief that development under capitalism may resolve the contradictions of dependency in backward nations overlooks the force of international capital, technology, and markets. In spite of the above shortcomings, dependency theory provides some tools which are helpful for understanding underdevelopment in the third-world.

The subsequent sections will attempt to make some comparisons of the three major comparative traditions (Marx, Weber, and the dependency school) to the ideas of Nkrumah.

Nkrumah's Notions of the
Global Context/Theory of Development

The systematic analytical writing about the political thought of leaders of underdeveloped countries has not received adequate attention.[25] Yet, African statesmen and politicians have been very vocal about the political, social, and particularly economic development of their nations. Although the subject of development was not talked about as frequently as questions relating to nationalism, imperialism, and colonial rule, its discussion has gained momentum. This is because, after political independence, the obvious concern of leaders of underdeveloped nations has been economic development as well. Consequently, African explanations of underdevelopment are inextricably linked with ideas on nationalism, imperialism, and colonialism. And, in spite of the diversity in African political and historical experiences, there are major recurrent themes which are shared by a vast number of influential African politicians.

Nkrumah's ideas and attitudes on underdevelopment in Ghana and

Africa generally are well detailed in his autobiographical accounts, speeches, articles, party pamphlets, policy statements, and reports. It is also significant that as President of the first black African state to gain political independence, his theoretical ideas on this subject have contributed in some degree to the formation of ideas and actions of both the ruling and the ruled of the African continent.

It is from these standpoints that I analyze the views of Nkrumah regarding African underdevelopment and particularly Ghanaian underdevelopment. In pursuit of this task, I will discuss Nkrumah's notions of how the global economy affects African and Ghanaian underdevelopment. In this connection, two main themes will be analyzed–neocolonialism and dependency perspectives. Since these two theories are so closely interrelated thematically, various comparison of the ideas involved will be made whenever appropriate.

Neocolonialism, Dependency, and Nkrumah

In dealing with countries outside Africa, Nkrumah embarked upon a policy of "positive neutralism" as he put it. What Nkrumah meant was that he did not want Ghana or any other African country to get involved in the cold war.[26]

An extension of Nkrumah's "positive neutralism" was what he referred to as "Neocolonialism." To him, "Neocolonialism" was the condition where a state may be politically independent but dependent economically on other states. Dependency, on the other hand, was the situation that the history of colonial imperialism has left and that modern imperialism creates in underdeveloped countries. According to dependency theory, the world is divided into centers and peripheries, with gains from international transactions always in favor of the developed center states.

In a 1960 speech, Nkrumah declared: "We must not be so preoccupied with the urgent problems of political independence as to overlook a scarcely less vital sphere–the economic sphere. Yet it is here more than anything else, that we must look for the schemings of a politically frustrated colonialism." [27]Here, Nkrumah was giving a warning about neocolonialism.

Also in his "*I Speak of Freedom,*"he wrote that:

> ...*the colonial powers and their imperialist allies are beginning to advance a new, subtle theory–and a disguised one, at that–to safeguard their position in Africa and to beguile and bamboozle Africans. They are prepared to grant*

political independence, but at the same time, they are also planning to continue to dominate the African territories in the economic field by establishing control over the economic life of the newly independent African countries. There is no difference between political imperialism and economic imperialism.[28]

Elsewhere, Nkrumah referred to neocolonialism as "the process of handing independence over to the African people with one hand, only to take it away with the other hand"; he defined it as

clientele sovereignty or fake independence; namely, the practice of granting a sort of independence by the metropolitan power, with the concealed intention of making the liberated country a client-state and controlling it effectively by means other than political ones.[29]

Also, in his *Neocolonialism: The Last Stage of Imperialism,* Nkrumah wrote that: "...Neocolonialism is the worse form of imperialism. For those who practice it, it means power without responsibility and for those who suffer from it, it means exploitation without redress."[30] What Nkrumah is arguing about here is that under imperialism, there was something like public accountability but this is lacking in neocolonial imperialism.

From the foregoing quotations, a number of themes do emerge. Firstly, Nkrumah advanced the argument that the major aim of neocolonialists was economic domination. Secondly, Nkrumah seemed to be saying that the economic exploitation created a dependency situation which makes the less developed countries depend, especially, economically on the developed countries.

Even though Nkrumah viewed neocolonialism as a form of economic exploitation, he recognized that neocolonialists did not confine their operation to the economic sphere. For example, the neocolonialists send expatriate teachers to the independent states who according to Nkrumah, do act as "cultural ambassadors" by influencing the minds of the young against their own country.[31]

For Nkrumah to look at underdevelopment in terms of one group (rich) exploiting the other (poor), he seems to agree with the structuralist dependency perspective which explains underdevelopment as a consequence of the center (rich nations) exploiting the periphery (poor nations). In order to better understand Nkrumah's view on imperialism, we need to examine Nkrumah's view in relation to Lenin.

Lenin also offers some explanations as to how imperialism works. Imperialism, according to Lenin, arises out of the necessity of capitalist societies to "export" their capital to foreign outlets for investment. And like Lenin, Nkrumah echoes the exploitive tendencies of "export" capital which involves the exploitation of labor and riches of less developed countries.[32] Moreover, Nkrumah cherished the notion that at the center of neocolonialism lies the multinational corporations, Thus, the multinational corporations do engage in economic activities which tend to exploit the less developed countries and therefore inhibit development. Nkrumah believed that because the presence of colonial powers necessarily means subjugation and exploitation of indigenous Africans, it is necessary to abolish and eliminate all vestiges of colonialism (including neocolonialism) which have prevented development.

Also, like Lenin, Nkrumah believed that imperialism was the inevitable consequence of the capitalist system. Nkrumah moved back and forth between this position and the view that colonies and imperialism were not necessarily "the highest stage of capitalism," but rather the result of policy choices made by imperialistic governments. (It is not only Nkrumah who oscillates between these two views. Kenneth Grundy observed that the leaders of Mali, Modibo Keita, and Guinea, Sekou Toure follow the Leninist interpretation with a few modifications while the politicians in Senegal, Ivory Coast, and Nigeria largely view imperialism as a policy that could be pursued by any nation or group of nations, and not necessarily capitalist in a certain transformation or evolutionary stage.) [33]

In summary, Nkrumah views underdevelopment as a result of imperialism. Imperialists, in Nkrumah's mind, have cleverly postponed their ultimate demise by deviously granting formal independence to their colonies, yet by various economic and political devices, continue to exploit and direct the fortunes of the new states. Also, to Nkrumah, the essence of neocolonialism is that the state which is subject to it is, in theory, independent and has all the outward trappings of international sovereignty; but in reality its economic system and thus its political policy is directed from outside. Here, Nkrumah recognizes the relationship between economics and politics.

Moreover, Nkrumah recognized that the result of neocolonialism is that foreign capital is used for the exploitation of the less developed areas. Also, Nkrumah embraces Lenin's conception of imperialism, including its inevitability and its exclusive association with capitalism.

Nkrumah borrowed from Marx and Lenin and he improvised in applying those ideas to Ghana. Improvisations resulted in certain inconsistencies in relation to Lenin's theory of imperialism and other classical Marxist ideas. All the same, Nkrumah considered himself a Marxist theorist. This did not mean that he was in total agreement with Marxist theory. At best, Nkrumah may be characterized as a syncretic theorist who used Marxist political thought giving it an African expression.

Nkrumah's anti-imperialist, anti-capitalist posture, and his view of the exploitation of the less developed nations by industrialized states have been echoed by the dependency theorists. Thus, like the dependency school, Nkrumah sees underdevelopment as caused by external rather than internal forces.

It is clear that Nkrumah was wary of capitalist presence in Africa. He never meant the exclusion of foreign capital from operating in less developed countries. His struggle against neocolonialism was aimed at preventing the financial power of the developed countries being used in such a way as to impoverish the less developed. Thus, to Nkrumah, national and continental development based on freedom from foreign domination in any form is the first order of business. For Nkrumah an unacceptable foreign investment is one that dominates and exploits the Ghanaians. Yet, the specifics of justifiable rate of return as a way of measuring exploitive and non-exploitive investment cannot be determined. The next section will address Nkrumah's views related to the national political responses to the development problem.

Nkrumah's Views Related to the National Political Responses to the Development Problem

In the preceding section, we analyzed Nkrumah's notions of how the global economy affects development. In this section, our objective is to analyze Nkrumah's proposals for the political and economic transformation of Ghana. To tackle the development problem, Nkrumah saw the urgency of firstly attaining political independence through a non-violent approach. Once political independence is achieved, according to Nkrumah, economic development would follow if the nation follows some arrangements. Specifically, Nkrumah suggests the need for a one-party system, the need for state-controlled classless society, the need to pursue socialism and planned economy and, finally, the need for a unified Africa. These themes will now be discussed.

Necessity of Political Independence

According to Nkrumah, the colonial powers were responsible for Ghana's social, economic, cultural, and political backwardness, and so the first step in tackling the issue of African underdevelopment was liquidation of colonialism to gain independence. Nkrumah made this very clear in his words, "See ye first the political kingdom and all other things will be added unto it." This injunction was inscribed on the base of Nkrumah's statue in the capital, Accra.

Elsewhere, Nkrumah highlighted this same idea by saying: "And everywhere men and women are beginning to search consciously for political means to resolve their problems and advance their hopes."[34]   On this same issue, Martin L. Kilson quoted Nkrumah as saying: "This country must progress politically—indeed political self-determination is the means of further realization of our social, economic, and cultural potentialities. It is political freedom that dictates the pace of economic and social progress."[35] What Nkrumah was saying was that when a country becomes politically independent, it was better able to direct its economic objectives as well. This seems to be a contradiction of Nkrumah's own notion of neocolonialism. By neocolonialism, Nkrumah brought out the point that when a country becomes independent politically, it still continued to be dependent economically on advanced states. Despite this contradiction, Nkrumah still believed the first step towards modernization is political independence.

If the first objective in order to surmount a state of underdevelopment is political independence, how can political independence be achieved? According to Nkrumah, the first stage of the struggle for independence called for the formation of the political party. Specifically, he believed that the vehicle for independence is one-party mass movement.[36] Nkrumah's notion of the role of the party as an agent of social change will be discussed later.

It was Nkrumah's understanding that colonial powers rarely surrender power and political control voluntarily. He made this point clear when he wrote in his *Autobiography* that freedom therefore becomes a product of "bitter and vigorous struggle."[37]   He also estimated that "...a people's readiness and willingness to assume the responsibilities of self-rule is the criterion of their preparedness to undertake those responsibilities." [38]

Nkrumah believed that this pressure for political independence should take the form of "Positive Action," an idea he borrowed from George Padmore. [39] By "Positive Action," Nkrumah meant that his party, the Convention Peoples' Party (CPP), was going to follow the "Gandhian non-violent" approach to achieve political independence. The weapons were political agitation, newspaper, and educational campaigns, and as a last resort, application of strikes, boycotts, and non-cooperation, all of which were based on the principle of non-violence. [40] It seemed there is a contradiction in the meaning of "Positive Action," for Nkrumah was quoted elsewhere to have said that freedom has never been handed over to a colonial people on a silver platter, "...it had been won only after bitter struggles." [41]

"Tactical Action," on the other hand, is a compromising approach adopted by Nkrumah to lead the Gold Coast to political independence. "Tactical Action" was a strategy where Nkrumah cooperated with the colonial power while still adhering to the aim of fighting for political independence. [42] The CPP became Nkrumah's political party, the vehicle for carrying out the strategies of "Positive Action" and "Tactical Action." (In this connection, it must also be noted that while the United Gold Coast Convention, UGCC, the first Gold Coast nationalist party believed in "independence at the earliest possible time," Nkrumah and his CPP agitated for "independence now.") [43]

It must be borne in mind that Nkrumah's reliance on non-violent methods of political action does not mean that he was a pacifist by choice. It merely meant that, after accurate assessment of the realities of the British force in Africa, Nkrumah was convinced that it would be suicidal for the independence movement to engage in any form of physical confrontation with the stronger colonial power. Consequently, Nkrumah was compelled to use non-violent approaches. This does not mean that the threat or possibility of violence was totally absent. In fact, the presence of the threat of violence tended to temper the British response to nationalist demands.

After utilizing the "Positive Action" and "Tactical Action" strategies (both of which followed the Gandhian non-violent approach) to achieve independence, Nkrumah suggested what was to be done to ensure sound political and economic transformation.

The Role of the Party as an Agent of Social Change

In his speech at the Accra Arena to celebrate the tenth anniversary of the founding of the CPP on June 12, 1959, Nkrumah defined the aim of the CPP in the context of the overall transformation of Ghanaian society: "The aim of our party is to develop our economy, modernize our agriculture, and industrialize Ghana from a system of colonial economy and create a system of independent economy."[44]

In the process of social transformation and political development in Ghana, Nkrumah envisioned the CPP as the vanguard of the people and categorically stated that "The Convention Peoples' Party is Ghana. Our Party not only provides the Government but is also the custodian which stands guard over the welfare of the people."[45] In essence, Nkrumah seemed to be suggesting that the CPP is the concrete expression of the broad masses of the people. What is being denied here is the existence of an opposition party as well as the self-restraint of the party. The exclusion of opposition interest is more of a Leninist than a Weberian contention which emphasizes the need to accommodate diverse and opposing interests.

Other underlying principles were evident in Nkrumah's concept of the party in the process of social change. According to Nkrumah, the organizational principle of the party must be based on "democratic centralism." In the party all must be equal regardless of race or tribe and must be free to express their views. "But once a majority decision is taken, we expect such a decision to be loyally executed, even by those who must have opposed the decision."[46] This closely follows Lenin's notion of democratic centralism which shaped party structure and practice. Attributed to Lenin, the theory of democratic centralism posits that no individual is to be greater than the party. Individual opinions are to be subordinated to the decisions of the majority.

Theoretically, the operation of democratic centralism is quite simple. Democratic centralism is composed of two parts, democracy and centralism. All responsible CPP officials are to be directly and freely chosen by party members at each level. All programs are to be openly discussed and, until a decision is reached, each member should be free to speak his mind. Once a decision is reached by majority vote, it is binding on all members. Thus, every member is to be subject to the authority and discipline of the party. This resembles the notion of "collective responsibility" in the British parliamentary system. The centralist aspects portray the right of higher body to make decisions for those below it.[47]

In practice, aspects of democratic centralism became less evident as Nkrumah consolidated himself in power.[48] The lines of communication became clogged as most decisions were reached at the top and handed down to regional and local bodies for implementation. Moreover, intra-party democracy was sacrificed in the name of party and national unity. Also, in most cases, party officials were imposed on the people affected. The officials became subservient tools which the CPP used to manipulate the populace.

Another principle of Nkrumah's notion of the CPP as an agent of social change was the emphasis on the supremacy of the CPP over all other functional institutions in Ghana.[49] Thus, in all things political, the CPP must be given priority because it is the revolutionary vanguard of the people and the only effective agent of social transformation. This implies that in the process of social transformation, the state or government is but a handmaiden of the CPP.

Thus far, we have stated that there are similarities of Nkrumah and Lenin's conception of the structure and the role of a party. The similarities are apparent in their concepts of the vanguard party within a society, "democratic centralism," and their overall view of the one-party state. On the other hand, Nkrumah departed from Lenin in regarding the CPP as a mass party. It was not an elite group. The CPP recruited the people rather than simply ruling in their name.

Despite the obvious contradictions of the theory and practice of Nkrumah's notion of the CPP and his apparent failure to use the CPP as the vehicle of social change, we cannot minimize the contribution of the CPP toward the eventual detribalization of Ghana. Contrary to the popularly held view of Nkrumah as a dictator, his view of the party as the vanguard of the people and as the only instrument of meaningful transformation in Ghana is a more persuasive view. A one-party system in transitional societies is designed to bring about a genuine unity of a country, otherwise diversified. Undoubtedly, Nkrumah was in opposition to the existence of classes in African societies, as for him classes divided rather than united people. The next section will be devoted to Nkrumah's analysis of the class question.

Nkrumah's Notion of the Class Question

Nkrumah defines class as: "...a sum total of individuals bound together by certain interests which as a class they try to preserve and protect."[50]

He believed that in a socialist state, the state represents workers and peasants, whereas in capitalist states, the state represents the exploiting class.[51] And, according to Nkrumah, in a non-socialist state, there are two main categories of class–the ruling class or classes and the subject class or classes. He saw the ruling class as possessing the major instruments of economic production and distribution, and the means of establishing its political dominance; while the subject class serves the interest of the ruling class, and is politically and economically dominated by it.[52] Thus, like Marx, Nkrumah saw conflict between the ruling class and the exploited class; and that the exploitation results from the development of productive forces.

In many respects, Nkrumah borrowed heavily from Marxist-Leninist writings. But it is important to state that Nkrumah, in the most part, diverges from Marx and Lenin on the question of social classes and the class struggle. Nkrumah quoted a prominent Gold Coast lawyer, John Mensah Sarbah, who romantically described the African traditional social order in these terms: "In the African social system the formation of pauper class is unknown, nor is there antagonism of class against class."[53] Similar views still exist in most parts of Africa. Furthermore, a rationale based on "classlessness" is employed by Africa's leaders to justify single-party rule, repression of dissent elements in society and to explain and defend policies of African socialism.[54] Thus, to Nkrumah, a single-party state denotes classlessness. Nkrumah went on to indicate that the single-party state denotes classlessness only if the state represents political power held by the people.[55] According to Nkrumah, just like Marx, the state then, is the expression of the domination of one class over the other. Thus, Nkrumah cherished the Marxian notion that the state does not represent all the people, rich and poor.

Nkrumah went on to state that where two or more parties exist there will be sharp cleavages because parties tend to represent certain class interests.[56] Nkrumah is in dissonance with Weber who stresses that the state ensures the sanctioning of a plurality of interests. Thus, while Weber recognizes the existence of different groups competing for power, Nkrumah, like Marx, stresses the domination of the exploitation of one class by another.

Like other Marxist Africans, Nkrumah shares the notion that class stratification in African is essentially a product of the internationalism of capital. Nkrumah like other African writers in the Marxist tradition refers to the spirit of brotherhood, and the communal organization of pre-capitalist societies in Africa as justification for their claim that contemporary forms of class antagonism in Africa; greed, corruption and privatization of profits and party politics were introduced alongside with imperialist penetration.[57]

The interpretation that traditional African societies were classless seems to be an exaggeration. Nkrumah admitted that in traditional African societies, there were chiefs and subjects but he noted that the chiefs were controlled by counselors and were removable. Thus he argues that these two classes were not antagonistic because there were controls built into the system to ensure proper behavior; and above all, property was communally owned. Thus, in the communalist social setting, it was impossible for social classes to develop. Viewing the class struggle in Marxian terms, in order for a class struggle to arise, society must be divided into antagonistic classes. (It must be noted that the basis for social classes in Ghana is the ownership of means of production. However, the land belonged to the people of the village. The chief merely apportioned the land among the villagers.) But there are other observers (including Nkrumah) who believe that as property relationships emerged and communalism gave way to slavery, feudalism, and capitalism, the class struggle began.[58]

Also, elsewhere, Nkrumah listed the composition of the agrarian social strata as consisting of plantation owners, absentee landlords and large property farm owners as constituting the exploiting group with the peasants and the rural proletariat as the exploited groups.[59] Here too, Nkrumah emphasized the point that the African peasantry has been exploited and suffered from imperialist-capitalist exploitation.

Furthermore, Professor Kenneth W. Grundy wrote that:

> European middle classes have traditionally been property-owning elements with a solid economic base for their social status. The main component of the rudimentary middle classes in the underdeveloped countries, however, is the bureaucratic intelligentsia. [60]

Intelligentsia here refers to any African who was educated in the West or East. There were three categories of the intelligentsia. First, there were those who supported the new privileged indigenous class, and they were also allies of imperialism and neocolonialism. They were anti-socialists, anti-communist and supported capitalist political and economic values. The second group advocated a mixed economy as a road towards socialism; while the third group supported and led the worker-peasant struggle for an all-out socialism.[61]

It is significant that Nkrumah disagreed with the notion that African classes are in their formative stages. He advanced the argument that although the African bourgeoisie is small numerically, and lacks financial support, it has close ties with foreign finance capital and business interest as many of the African bourgeoisie were employed by foreign firms. [62] Thus, the African bourgeoisie were mesmerized by capitalist institutions and organizations as they did have direct financial stake in the continuance of the foreign exploitation of Africa. This notion of Nkrumah is more of a Leninist perspective which emphasizes the exploitation of the colonies by the metropolitan power.

Moreover, the anti-colonialist and anti-imperialist struggle also reflects Nkrumah's conception of class. He equated all underdeveloped nations with the proletariat, and the colonialists as the bourgeoisie. In the colonialist situation, Gold Coast workers were regarded as the exploited class, while foreign firms and foreign planters (the British) were the exploiters. To overthrow foreign exploitation, Gold Coast nationalism was essential. Nkrumah admits that the intelligentsia always leads the nationalist movement.[63] This clearly indicates that, within the Gold Coast, there were indigenous classes, such as the intelligentsia and the peasants. Even though the intelligentsia does not control the means of production, they are still to be considered a social class. They control information. Furthermore, the case can be made that the intelligentsia take part in the exploitation of the people through corrupt practices, such as the embezzlement of public funds.

One significant point worth noting is that Nkrumah lumped together all Europeans as "haves" or exploiting class and all Africans as "have-nots" or exploited class regardless of their individual status within each nation. Unlike Lenin, Nkrumah made no effort to call upon class allies in European countries for assistance in the struggle, despite the possibility that Europeans might align themselves with their own class allies in African countries.

Grundy is not all that surprised by African leaders' rejection of antagonistic social classes because Grundy believes that this is a common device utilized by leaders to eliminate friction in their regimes. This device is what Talcott Parsons refers to as "cognitive distortions of ideologies."[64] From the standpoint of ruling groups, ideologies are used to integrate the social system. And because social classes present an element of division and disintegration in the social system, there is the tendency for the leaders to minimize the importance of social classes. When they do employ class analysis in African political life, they quickly portray it as a modern feature which was introduced along with internationalism of capital and therefore alien. Nkrumah subscribed to this contention.

However, the argument can be made that there were class stratifications in Africa even before the advent of capitalism. There existed in traditional Africa political, religious, and ascribed role differentials. For instance, the chieftaincy class, the medicine priests and priestesses and diviners certainly enjoyed a higher status than the ordinary person. Besides, there were those considered wealthy or poor. A major feature of traditional African class categories was that the rich did not own the means of production; and so they did not constitute a social class. This distinguishes the traditional African class categories from those in capitalist systems. The chiefs acted as a social class for the chiefs could exploit the subjects but this was culturally acceptable. So to completely deny that the African traditional society contained classes is to ignore all these social differentiations.

Dr. Ivan Potekhin, a prominent Russian Africanist, challenged the claim by African statesmen, including Nkrumah, that African society is largely classless.[65] Potekhin employed the Marxist historical and economic analysis to make the point that there is a widening gap between the African national bourgeoisie and the developing proletariat. A class-conscious proletariat, he maintained, is necessary for the transition to a socialist state.[66] It must be clarified that Nkrumah does not deny the existence of classes in African societies; rather he denied the existence of Marxist-Leninist class struggle by insisting that Africa could avoid class antagonisms. Nkrumah's denial of class antagonisms is attributable to his contention that classes have the tendency of dividing Africans. In fact, Ghana had a mixed economy but Nkrumah denied private ownership.

In essence, Nkrumah is making the case that a country can become socialist without having to go through the other stages, the characteristic of which is the presence of antagonistic classes. Thus, Nkrumah rejects the notion of Potekhin that capitalism is a stage African countries have to confront. If Nkrumah accepted Potekhin's thesis, it also meant his acceptance of antagonistic classes which is a fundamental attribute of capitalism. Therefore, Nkrumah completely denied that some day there may be conflict between the elites and peasantry. By so doing, Nkrumah denied the relevance of Marxist-Leninist class struggle. One may argue, however, that Potekhin and other Soviet writers are looking beyond the pre-independence unity and solidarity in traditional Africa to a future day when class conflicts could characterize the normal pattern of Africa's search for political development. What path then can most effectively and efficiently secure rapid development? This will be the focus of the next section.

Socialism and Planned Economy

In December, 1958, the All-African People's Conference (AAPC) held their first meeting in Accra and it was at this meeting that Nkrumah set forth four principles as the aims of the AAPC: national independence for the rest of Africa, national consolidation, the creation of transnational unity and community, and economic and social reconstruction. Social reconstruction, he said, had to be free of all foreign influences and must be "on the basis of African socialism." The economic and social reconstruction of Africa along African socialist lines was, therefore, to be the last phase of Pan-Africanist movement that started at the turn of the century with men like George Padmore, Marcus Garvey, W.E.B. DuBois, and Henry Sylvester Williams. African statesmen like Nkrumah, Toure, Senghor, and Kaunda all spoke of socialism in Africa as a revolutionary tool for Africa's independence and beyond that, socioeconomic reconstruction. Thus, the theme of social reconstruction through the establishment of a socialist economic system was a post-colonial priority for Nkrumah. For a better understanding of Nkrumah's socialism, I will attempt to discuss: a) the general concept of socialism; b) third-world and African socialism; and c) Nkrumah's socialism.

What is Socialism? Socialism is a concept which has many different definitions. According to Plano and Greenberg, socialism is:

A doctrine that advocates economic collectivism, seeking collective or governmental ownership of the means of production and distribution of goods. Its basic aims are to replace competition for profit by cooperation and social responsibility and to secure a more equitable distribution of income and opportunity.[67]

Thus, socialism is an economic system where government plays a major role in the production and distribution of goods and services.

Although the concept of socialism is definite in principle, it is very flexible in form depending on what country is applying it. Even though countries apply socialism differently, they seem to agree on the principle of more social ownership of almost all economic activities. The Soviet Union was an example of socialist economy with nearly all the economic activities controlled by the government. The U.S. is more of a capitalist society, but there are some tendencies toward socialism in the form of government welfare and other programs.

Third-World Perceptions on Socialism. Most third-world countries label themselves socialist, and by that label they mean a wide variety of things. All the same, there is one area in which there is complete agreement–the rejection of capitalism. The reason for the rejection of capitalism lies in the association of capitalism with colonialism and neocolonialism, both of which are exploitive.[68] Capitalism is rejected in principle because the capitalists were the colonial rulers who dominated the economies.

Third world rejects both capitalism and communism because it wants to avoid being pawns in the East-West struggle and wants to develop its economies free from outside control. Hence, the developing nations are most likely to accept socialism.

There seems to be a reasonable degree of consensus among scholars that third-world leaders tend to be socialistic in outlook. Edward Shils believes that these leaders promote policies which aim at creating socialistic, governmentally controlled enterprises, thereby discouraging capitalism.[69] James A. McCain also writes that third-world leaders adopt socialism in their effort to bring about a successful economic and industrial policy.[70] This same view has been expressed by William A. Friedland and Carl G. Rosberg.[71] David Apter looked at third-world leaders' interests in socialist activities as a way to produce greater efficiency and better motivation to work.[72]

Third-world leaders tend to find socialism appealing for the following reasons:

1. Third-world leaders believe that for development to occur, socialism should be based on government control of industries;
2. As a system based on morality, it discourages exploitation through

private ownership, while at the same time it allows individual incentive through limited ownership;

3. It is anti-imperialist;

4. It is anti-privileged; and

5. It is a system that enforces socially desirable activities, thereby ensuring social progress.[73]

Jomo Kenyatta, former Kenyan leader, discussed socialism by saying:

African socialism must draw on African traditions, must be adaptable to new and rapidly changing circumstances, and must not rest on a satellite relationship with any other country or bloc....[74]

All the same, Kenyatta encouraged foreign participation in the economic sector insofar as the foreign ventures did not dominate the economic sector.

What Did Nkrumah Mean by Socialism?   Like other third-world leaders, Nkrumah believed that socialism is "the only key to human progress."[75] Thus, he views socialism as the ultimate form of economic organization. And, while other African nationalists stress the continuity between traditional African social organizations and modern socialism to defend socialism, Nkrumah largely emphasizes the modernizing aspects of socialism. Occasionally, however, he looks to the past as well to justify socialism in Africa.

Nkrumah is quoted in the *African Institute Bulletin* that, "there is no such thing as African socialism. There is only scientific socialism which is valid the world over and we are building our society on the basis of scientific socialism."[76] By stressing the materialist outlook, Nkrumah argued that his position was scientific because that outlook is subject to objective scientific analysis and laws; it behaves in a predictable manner. This idea was borrowed from Marx. Thus, according to Nkrumah, socialism is the outcome of dialectical material process and therefore a science.

It must be noted that Nkrumah's socialism was not an ideological blueprint, but rather it was a pragmatic program. The principles of his socialism included:

1. Rejection of private capital as the major producer of goods and services;

2. Rejection of gross class inequalities in income and status;
3. Rejection of foreign monopolies (anti-imperialist);
4. Government control over most of the wealth as well as its distribution;
5. Need for national economic planning; and
6. Development of social services (welfare state based on production for use, not profit).[77]

Several themes do emerge from the above principles of Nkrumah's views on socialism. A major theme that stands out is Nkrumah's notion that the state should control the productive forces in society. This was a Marxian contention. To Nkrumah, state control was natural because, to him, the main economic resources in pre-capitalist African societies were communally owned. Thus, he looked to the past to justify his socialism. Drawing such a simple analogy shows a failure of Nkrumah to appreciate that the socioeconomic environment in traditional Africa with land abundance was very different from that of post-independence period which has the characteristics of science and technological development. Also, Nkrumah could justify the claim that only state control and distribution of resources would be equitable by his reference to how land was distributed in traditional African societies. In most traditional African societies, the chief did not lease out the land. The land belonged autonomously to the different families that made up the tribal unit. And, until recently, all members of each family unit had automatic access to the land.

Nkrumah's notion of central planning expanded his power. Even though Nkrumah cited the necessity of dialectical juxtaposition of views in his scientific socialism, he failed to allow the dialectical juxtaposition of views to operate. Even in the traditional societies of Africa, effective internal dialectics was in place. Decision was not the arbitrary privilege of a chief. Decision, usually followed by majority agreement, did not necessarily imply unanimity of thought. But rather decisions emerged only after very heated debates in which opposing views of the various elders were weighted intellectually. This provided possibilities of persuasion and finally consensus. Theoretically, Nkrumah's intellectual position on decision-making related with this traditional process. But in practice, for the most part, Nkrumah deviated from this intellectual conception and quelled the opposition in the decision-making process.

Moreover, Nkrumah cited the concept of tribal solidarity to bolster and defend both his central economic planning and his one-party system, all of which were meant to enhance his socialist development approach. And, to Nkrumah, tribal solidarity could be extended into national unity in which the state has authority and total control. Using Apter's thesis on ethnic solidarity, the case can be made that sacred concepts of taboos and superstitions which fostered tribal solidarity have become weak tools in the modern era.[78] To still ensure this kind of tribal solidarity and unity, Nkrumah substituted the sacred concepts of taboos and superstitions with force to throttle dissent.

Another major theme that arises from Nkrumah's socialism is his rejection of imperialism. Thus, he rejected foreign monopolies. (See Chapter 4 for analysis of how Nkrumah discouraged foreign monopolies.) It must be stated that Nkrumah was not so optimistic about self-propelled economic growth on solely Ghanaian initiative. He insisted that Ghana needed investments in the form of foreign capital. He even assured foreign firms of his government's preparedness to take sound measures to ensure their protection. It became an official doctrine which was clearly spelled out in the Ghanaian constitution. This legal document was meant to guarantee adequate compensation to foreign firms.[79]

Understandably, a legal instrument is a weak reed on which to base investments in Ghana. Even though Nkrumah gave assurances that nationalization was not in sight, he later nationalized some foreign firms. This matter will be detailed alter.

Nkrumah wanted some foreign capital, but at the same time, he objected to the heavy reliance on foreign capital as he believed that might render Ghana both economically and politically dependent on expatriate industry which will imply the introduction of colonization in another guise. Here too, his fear of neocolonialism is made abundantly clear.

Furthermore, Nkrumah believed that heavy reliance on foreign loans and credits as a method to finance industrialization simply postpones the growth of native industry. For this reason, Nkrumah also pushed for the need to rely, to some extent, on Ghana's own resources too build essential industries. In this capacity, Nkrumah embarked on a policy of "Ghanaianization" of the public service.[80] The desire to supplant foreign civil service was not an irrational one. By removing European officials, it became clear to Ghanaians that all posts were open to competent and qualified Ghanaians. Today, "Ghanaianization" is practically complete.

And it is clear that Nkrumah's support for "Ghanaianization" may well be related to his fear of neocolonialism and dependency.

Without question, Nkrumah's desire to encourage foreign investment and his statements that the last vestiges of colonialism must be eliminated, in my estimation, is not theoretically consistent. Yes, foreign businesses are remnants of the colonial past, but equally true is the fact that if Ghanaian economic and political development is to be enhanced, foreign aid in some form is essential. Nkrumah did not deny this. Even though he claimed to be an anti-imperialist but because of the lack of capital and other resources needed for his socialist revolution, he gave room to foreign investments as long as they did not try to exploit or dominate the country. And as stated earlier in this chapter, it is difficult to determine what constitutes a non-exploitive investment. This is because specifics of justifiable rate of return cannot be determined.

In conclusion, it can be said that Nkrumah meant well to develop Ghana by way of socialism. At the same time, Nkrumah sought to legitimize the central role of the state in the national economic development. By legitimizing the need for state ownership of the means of production and distribution, and also introducing a centrally planned economy, Nkrumah increased his own power. He did all he could to discourage the formation of competing power centers springing from independent private economic foundations as these could grow to the extent of becoming a rival power to his and the Convention Peoples Party's (CPP) prestige. Thus, Nkrumah realized that the control of the state economic machinery could protect and preserve his own power and security. And, as it will be seen later, his power was only protected in the short-run; as in the long-run, he was overthrown.

Nkrumah's Views on Pan-Africanism
In keeping with the theme of concentrating powers to meet all real and potential problems, Nkrumah's consistent goal had been the establishment of an all-African continental government. Using the twin examples of the success and achievements of the United States and Soviet Union, Nkrumah uncompromisingly advocated for political union rather than economic cooperation advocated by the majority of Africa's leaders.[81]

The above clearly indicates that, in an important sense, Nkrumah had not really retreated from a doctrine of the primacy of politics. When he said, "Seek ye first the political kingdom," he did not seem to have meant the

Ghanaian kingdom on its own. In the context of his political philosophy as a whole, the real political kingdom for Africa is the kingdom of Africa itself. This is made clear in his words: "The independence of Ghana is meaningless unless it is linked up with the total liberation of the African continent."[82]

Moreover, Nkrumah believed that a balkanized Africa is vulnerable to the danger of being manipulated by outsiders.[83] This did not mean that political independence is useless without economic power, but rather, according to Nkrumah, political independence was weak without political unity. Thus, when political freedom was combined with and reinforced by political union, Africa would then be able to break the economic power that others have over her. And, in his book *Neocolonialism: The Last Stage of Imperialism*, Nkrumah argues that the exploitation of Africa is itself carried out on a Pan-African basis. This is economic Pan-Africanism on the part of the exploiters. Nkrumah believes that it is only political Pan-Africanism on the part of the exploited that can break the hold of the continental monopolists. Specifically, he wrote that:

> *The foreign firms who exploit our resources long ago saw the strength to be gained from acting on a Pan-African scale. By means of interlocking dictatorships, cross-share holdings and other devices, groups of apparently different companies have formed, in fact, one enormous capitalist monopoly. The only effective way to challenge this economic empire and to recover possession of our heritage is for us to act on a Pan-African basis through a Union Government.[84]*

Thus, Nkrumah is arguing that the same way the imperialists united to exploit, the exploited must unite in order to withstand the oppression by the imperialists. Furthermore, he stated elsewhere that: "Without organizational strength we are weak; unity is the dynamic force behind any great venture."[85] He seemed to believe right up to his fall from power that an Africa disunited was, in a fundamental sense, an Africa disorganized.

For some years Nkrumah sought to establish himself as the leader of the African independence struggle and the Pan-African unity movement and met serious opposition from other African leaders. Specifically, other African leaders who were likewise sensitive and concerned for their state's security, were suspicious of Nkrumah's bid for leadership. To them, territorial sovereignty seemed a more reliable barrier to external control than government that could well come under the influence of hostile African as well as alien forces. Thus, to unify alone the lines of Nkrumah's demands would, without question, decrease their own personal powers and prestige. The fact that the Organization of African Unity's (OAU) charter contains a strong clause in defense of national sovereignty and the non-interference in internal affairs was an undoubted manifestation of the position of the majority of Africa's leaders. This illustrated well the unpopularity of Nkrumah's proposal of immediate sacrifice of national sovereignty in the name of African unity.

Summary and Conclusion

This chapter has attempted to provide some analysis of how Nkrumah viewed the Ghanaian and African underdevelopment problem and suggests what can be done to bring about development. By his references to such concepts as dependency, neocolonialism and imperialism, Nkrumah made the case that African underdevelopment is closely interconnected to the global economy. He saw economic exploitation as a major characteristic of the macro-economy.

And for Ghana and Africa to develop, Nkrumah came up with some propositions which are worth analyzing. As a first step towards development, Nkrumah stressed the need to become politically independent, and made this clear in the words "See ye first the political kingdom and all other things will be added unto it." Thus, to Nkrumah, it was no longer economic power that determined political relationships. On the contrary, Nkrumah came to argue that political power is the inescapable prerequisite to economic and social power.

All the same, Nkrumah was fearful of neocolonialism which emphasizes big powers control of poor countries' economies. By the concept of neocolonialism, Nkrumah made the point that political independence alone was not sufficient. He argued that the African attainment of sovereignty, when not accompanied by a change in economic relationships could give rise to what he called client states. The whole doctrine of neocolonialism seems to reassert afresh the proposition that real power lies, in the final analysis, with those who are economically powerful. Had Nkrumah now stumbled on to the fact that the "political kingdom" on its own lacked the power to "add things" to itself?

Partly because of its centralizing functions and also as a doctrine of mass involvement, Nkrumah adopted socialism as the route toward development. For true development, Nkrumah stressed the need for unity within Ghana and also on the continent. And since he viewed the two-party system and classes as having divisive tendencies, he pushed for a one-party system and discouraged the formation of another party and also denied the existence of antagonistic classes in Ghana. Undoubtedly, his scientific socialism stressed the state control of productive forces. All the same, he did not lose sight of the fact that Ghana lacked the capital and other resources necessary for development. Therefore, he encouraged foreign firms to invest insofar as they did not exploit or dominate Ghana. The point must also be made that through the centralization of authority, Nkrumah expanded his own power.

There was tension between Nkrumah the political theorist and Nkrumah the pragmatist. This resulted in many inconsistencies. Nkrumah might have been consistent or inconsistent but he was undeniably pragmatic.

Focusing on the same idea of centralization and unity, Nkrumah stressed the need for a united Africa as balkanized Africa made the continent vulnerable to control from outsiders.

It must be said that the understanding of these philosophies of Nkrumah will help us better understand the nature of his public policies which is discussed in Chapters 4 and 5. And based on the nature of Nkrumah's political thought discussed in this chapter, we should expect Nkrumah to embark on policies which emphasized the central role of the state. Moreover, we should also expect him to pursue policies that will be anti-imperialist and also anti-neocolonialist.

With this general discussion and analysis of the major frameworks for understanding Nkrumah in place, the next chapter will discuss his life and political career, particularly, before his accession of power. Discussion will also be pursued of the political, economic, and social legacy Nkrumah inherited.

Endnotes

[1] Karl Marx and Friedrich Engles, "Manifesto of the Communist Party," in Samuel H. Beer (ed.), *The Communist Manifesto* (New York: Appleton-Century-Crofts, Inc., 1985), p. 12.

[2] Ibid., pp. 16-17.

[3] Ibid, pp. 18-19.

[4] Marx never fully elaborated a theory of class. Only in the brief and incomplete last chapter of the third volume of *Capital* did he offer a conception: "Wage labourers, capitalists, and landowners constitute the three big classes of modern society based upon the capitalist mode of production" (1967, 3:885). However, Marx recognized the existence of other classes. He identified in *The Class Struggles in France, 1848-1850* and *The Eighteenth Brumaire of Louis Bonaparte,* classes such as the aristocracy, industrial bourgeoisie, petty bourgeoisie, peasantry, lumpen proletariat, industrial proletariat, bourgeois monarchy, and large bourgeoisie.

[5] Marx and Engels, "Manifesto of the Communist Party," p. 15.

[6] Ibid., pp. 14-16.

[7] Ibid., p. 13.

[8] V.I. Lenin, *Imperialism: The Highest Stage of Capitalism* (New York: International Publishers, 1939), p. 85.

[9] Max Weber, *From Max Weber: Essays in Sociology.* Translated and edited with an Introduction by H.H. Gerth and C. Wright Mills (New York: Oxford University Press, 1958) p. 78.

[10] Ibid., p. 181.

[11] Lenin, *Imperialism: The Highest Stage of Capitalism,* p. 85.

[12] Ronald H. Chilcote, *Theories of Comparative Politics: The Search for a Paradigm* (Boulder: Westview Press, 1981), pp. 297-298.

[13] Ronald H. Chilcote, *Theories of Development and Underdevelopment* (Boulder: Westview Press, 1984), pp. 23-25.

[14] Raul Prebisch, *Change and Development--Latin America's Great Task* (New York: Praeger Publishers, 1971), pp. 171-173; Peter H. Lindert and Charles P. Kindleberger, *International Economics* (Homewood, Illinois: Irwin, Inc., 1982), pp. 92-94.

[15] Osvado Sunkel, "Big Business and Dependencia," *Foreign Affairs,* 50 (April 1972), pp. 517-531.

[16] Celso Furtado, *Diagnosis of the Brazilian Crisis.* Translated by Suzette Macedo (Berkeley and Los Angeles: University of California Press, 1965), p. 61.

[17] Kenneth Waltz, "Theory of International Relations, in Fred I. Greenstein and Nelson W. Polsby, *Handbook of Political Science* (International Politics) (Menlo Park, CA: Addison-Wesley Publishing Company, 1975), pp. 26-31; also Johan Galtung, "A Structural Theory of Imperialism," *Journal of Peace Research,* 8 (1971), pp. 81-117.

[18] Chilcote, *Theories of Development and Underdevelopment,* p. 86.

[19] Pablo Gonzalez Casanova, *Democracy in Mexico.* Translated by Danielle Salti (New York: Oxford University Press, 1970), pp. 172-192.

[20] Fernando Henriqué Cardoso and Enzo Faletto, *Dependency and Development.* Translated by Marjory Mattingly Urquidi (Berkeley: University of California Press, 1979), p. ix.

[21] Ibid., p. x.

[22] Ibid., p. xx.

[23] Ibid., pp. xxi-xxii.

[24] Ibid., p. 55.

[25] Among the few exceptions are Thomas Hodgkin, "A Note on the Language of African Nationalism," in St. Anthony's Papers No. 10, *African Affairs: No. 1,* ed. by Kenneth Kirkwood (London, 1961), pp. 22-40; Immanuel Wallerstein, "The Political Ideology of the PDG," *Presence Africaine,* XII (First Quarter 1962), pp. 30-41; Henry L. Bretton, "Current Political Thought and Practice in Ghana," *American Political Science Review,* LII (March 1958), pp. 46-63; Walter Z. Laqueur, "Communism and Nationalism in Tropical Africa," Foreign Affairs, XXXIX (July 1961), pp. 610-621. For a brief explanation of ideas of African leaders, see Crawford Young, *Ideology and Development in Africa* (New Haven: Yale University Press, 1982), pp. 151-182.

[26] Dorothy Willner, "Community Leadership," United *Nations Series,* ST/SOA, Ser. 0/36 (1960), pp. 11-12.

[27] Kwame Nkrumah, "Positive Action in Africa,"in James Duffy and Robert A. Manners (eds.), *Africa Speaks* (New Jersey: Princeton University Press, 1961), p. 53.

[28] Kwame Nkrumah, *I Speak of Freedom: A Statement of African Ideology* (New York: Praeger Publishers, 1961), p. 200.

[29] Daniel A. Offiong, *Imperialism and Dependency: Obstacles to African Development* (Washington, D.C.: Howard University Press, 1982), p. 122.

[30] Kwame Nkrumah, *Neocolonialism: The Last Stage of Imperialism* (London: Nelson & Sons, 1965), p. 1.

[31] Ibid., p. 35.

[32] Ibid., pp. 35-36.

[33] Kenneth W. Grundy, "Marxism-Leninism and African Underdevelopment: The Malian Approach," *International Journal*, XVII (Summer 1962), pp. 300-304; for a more detailed examination of Guinean ideology, see Wallerstein, "The Political Ideology of the PDG," pp. 30-41.

[34] Kwame Nkrumah, "African Prospect," *Foreign Affairs*, XXXVII (October 1958), p. 45.

[35] Martin L. Kilson, Jr., "Nationalism and Social Classes in British West Africa," *Journal of Politics*, XX, No. 2 (May 1985), p. 380.

[36] Kenneth W. Grundy, "The Political Ideology of Kwame Nkrumah," *Monograph Series in World Affairs, Vol. 5,* Nos. 3 and 4 (University of Denver Publication, 1967-68), p. 78.

[37] Kwame Nkrumah, *The Autobiography of Kwame Nkrumah* (New York: Nelson and Sons, 1957), p. iii.

[38] Ibid., pp. 190-191.

[39] George Padmore, *The Gold Coast Revolution* (London: Dennis Dobson Ltd., 1963), pp. 79-80.

[40] Patrick Duncan, "Non-Violence at Accra," *Africa Today,* 6 (1959) pp. 30-33; Padmore, *The Gold Coast Revolution,* p. 80; also see particularly Kwame Nkrumah, "What I Mean by Positive Action," *Ghana Pamphlets,* No. 1 (Accra, 1949).

[41] Nkrumah, *The Autobiography of Kwame Nkrumah,* p. 92.

[42] W.G. Runciman, "Charismatic Legitimacy and One-Party Rule in Ghana," *European Journal of Sociology,* 4 (1963), pp. 148-165.

[43] Padmore, *The Gold Coast Revolution,* pp. 60-62; also pp. 67-71.

[44] Kwame Nkrumah, *Axioms of Kwame Nkrumah* (London: Nelson andSons, 1967), pp. 42-43.

[45] Ibid., p. 42.

[46] Kwame Nkrumah, *Speech at the Accra Arena to Celebrate the Tenth Anniversay of the Founding of the CPP,* June 12, 1959.

[47] Nkrumah, *I Speak of Freedom: A Statement of African Ideology,* p. 164.

[48] Grundy, "The Political Ideology of Kwame Nkrumah," p. 81.

[49] Speech made in Accra, June 12, 1960, cited in Nkrumah, *Axioms of Kwame Nkrumah*, p. 43.

[50] Kwame Nkrumah, *Class Struggle in Africa* (New York: International Publishers, 1970), p. 17.

[51] Ibid.

[52] Ibid.

[53] Quoted by Kwame Nkrumah, "The Future of African Law," in *Voice of Africa* (Accra, April 4, 1962), p. 14.

[54] Martin L. Kilson, "Authoritarian and Single-Party Tendencies in African Politics," *World Politics,* 15, No. 2 (January 1963), pp. 268-270.

[55] Nkrumah, *Class Struggle in Africa*, p. 18.

[56] Ibid.

[57] Ibid., pp. 13-22; also Kwame Nkrumah, *Consciencism: Philosophy and Ideology for Decolonization and Development* (New York: Monthly Review Press, 1964), p. 69.

[58] Nkrumah, *Class Struggle in Africa*, p. 13.

[59] Ibid., p. 76.

[60] Kenneth W. Grundy, "The Class Struggle in Africa: An Examination of Conflicting Theories," *The Journal of Modern African Studies,* 2, No. 3 (1964), p. 382; also Nkrumah, *Class Struggle in Africa*, p. 30.

[61] Nkrumah, *Class Struggle in Africa*, pp. 36-40.

[62] Ibid., pp. 10-12.

[63] Ibid., pp. 13, 18.

[64] Talcott Parsons, *The Social System* (Glencoe, Ill.: Free Press, 1951).

[65] I.I. Potekhin, "African Socialism: A Soviet View," in William H. Friedland and Carl G. Rosberg (eds.), *African Socialism* (Stanford: Stanford University Press, 1964), pp. 97-112.

[66] Ibid., p. 110.

[67] Jack C. Plano and Milton Greenberg, *The American Political Dictionary* (New York: Holt, Rinehart and Winston Inc., 1963), p. 14.

[68] Lyman Tower Sargent, *Contemporary Political Ideologies* (Homewood, Ill.: The Dorsey Press, 1984), p. 174.

[69] Edward Shils, "The Concentration and Dispersion of Charisma," *World Politics,* 11 (October 1958), pp. 6, 10.

[70] James A. McCain, "Attitudes Towards Socialism, Policy and Leadership in Ghana," *African Studies Review,* 22 (1979) p. 157.

[71] Friedland and Rosberg, *African Socialism,* p. 263.

[72] David Apter, "Nkrumah, Charisma and the Coup," *Daedalus,* 97 (Summer 1968), p. 764.

[73] Andrew Grant, *Socialism and the Middle Classes* (New York: International Publishers, Inc., 1959), pp. 52-60; also, see Helen Desfosses and Jacques Levesque, *Socialism in the Third World* (NewYork: Praeger Publishers, 1975), pp. 194, 205.

[74] "What Is African Socialism?" *African Institute Bulletin,* 3, No. 9 (September 1965), p. 223.

[75] See his speech to the Workers on May Day, 1965; reprinted in *Ghana Today,* IX, No. 5 (May 5, 1965), p. 2.

[76] "What Is African Socialism?" *African Institute Bulletin,* p. 223.

[77] Desfosses and Levesque, *Socialism in the Third World,* pp. 194, 204-205.

[78] David Apter, *The Politics of Modernization* (Chicago: The University of Chicago Press, 1965), pp. 32-38; also David Apter, *Ghana in Transition* (New York: Atheneum, 1963), pp. 104-105.

[79] Great Britain, Statutory Instruments (1957, No. 277), *The Ghana (Constitution) Order in Council* (1957), paragraph 54.

[80] *Ghana Today,* V (June 21, 1961), p. 3.

[81] His most comprehhensive argument for unity appears in his book *Africa Must Unite* (New York: Praeger Publishers, 1963). It must be made clear, however, that Nkrumah's advocacy of unity may be no more than a verbal advocacy, for it seems his desire for unity would only be uncompromising if he were to be the directing force. See also the two booklets published for the National Liberation Council for the Ghana Ministry of Information, *Nkrumah's Subversion in Africa* (Accra-Tema, 1966); and *Nkrumah's Deception of Africa* (Accra-Tema, 1967).

[82] Stephen Dzirasa, *Political Thought of Dr. Nkrumah* (Accra: Guinea Press, n.d.), p. 14.

[83] Grundy, "The Political Ideology of Kwame Nkrumah," p. 89.

[84] Nkrumah, *Neocolonialism: The Last Stage of Imperialism,* p. 259.

[85] Nkrumah, *I Speak of Freedom: A Statement of African Ideology,* p. 3.

Discussion Questions

1. Analyze the conceptual and practical relationships between "imperialism," "dependency," and "neocolonialism."

2. Do you see any major differences in the definition and analysis of the concept of "class" as identified by Marx, Lenin, and Nkrumah? Explain your response.

3. Contrast the tenets of Nkrumah with respect to "socialism," "scientific socialism," and "African socialism."

4. What solutions did Nkrumah suggest for the third-world's underdevelopment?

Chapter 3
Ghana and Nkrumah

To facilitate a better understanding of the subject, the first part of this chapter will focus primarily on the background of Ghana which Nkrumah inherited, emphasizing political, economic, and social conditions. The other part of the chapter will concentrate on the life and career of Nkrumah before his rise to power; and also an analysis of his political activities from the time of his return from London in 1947 until he became president in 1957. The knowledge of this historical dimension will be of great help in understanding the context of Nkrumah's leadership.

Ghana is a small West African country with a size of 91,843 square miles (about the size of Oregon) and a population of 15.6 million people. Many ethnic divisions exist in Ghana, with each having its own dialect. Prominent linguistic groups are the Akans, Ewes, and Gas. Major ethnic groups of the North comprise of the Gruma, Grusi, and Dagomba. The peoples of the Middle Belt are the Nkonya, Lolobi, and Bowli, while the South is composed of the Akan, Ewe, Ga, and Nzima.[1] About 20 percent of the population is Christian, 15 percent Muslim, with a majority having a firm belief in "fetishism."[2] The basic idea of "fetishism" is that the worshippers firmly believe that the only way God can be communicated with is through objects like stones, trees, lakes, and so forth. The worshippers have as their leader the fetish priest or priestess, who keeps the particular object in a shrine and occasionally paints it with blood of animals. The worshippers go to the shrine to pour libations and to seek appeasement from the dead and God to bestow blessings on them. They also worship their ancestors. Most of the idol and ancestor worshippers are uneducated and believe in the strict observance of sacrifices at the shrine. They have little or no respect for modern government other than for their own chiefs, who are mostly fetish priests or priestesses to the shrines.

Political and Social Conditions

The pre-colonial and colonial past of Ghana must be understood in order to have a better understanding of the politics and economy of the legacy Nkrumah inherited. Before Ghana was colonized, the Ghanaian kings, chiefs, and elders performed political, religious, economic, and social functions in their particular localities. But after the British occupation of the Gold Coast around 1844, the kings, chiefs, and elders lost some of those functions. After the British occupation, the British made conscious and deliberate attempts to govern the territories they had newly acquired, about which they were largely ignorant. Chieftaincy was central. The Ghanaian kings were both the political and religious leaders. The British lacked personnel to manage these new territories.[3] Lord Lugard, a British governor in Northern Nigeria came up with a partial solution. In 1920, he adopted the "Indirect Rule" system as a matter of practical expediency which he applied with pedantic vigor.[4] The "Indirect Rule" system was a kind of system by which the British ruled their newly acquired colonies through the existing traditional institutions. In pursuit of this policy, the British assigned the chiefs to expedite duties on their behalf by following specific principles laid down by the British. This does not mean that there were two rules, the British and the native; the British and the natives worked either separately or in cooperation, but there was just a single government in which the natives had well-defined duties and acknowledged status equally with British officials. Their duties never conflicted and there was little overlap. Since the chiefs were expediting duties for the British, attacks on the chiefs meant attacks on the British and perpetrators were punished. The main principles of the Indirect Rule system were as follows:

1. Chiefs did not have the power to raise or control armed forces;
2. Power to impose taxes was the preserve of the British Crown;
3. Appropriation of land was also not in the hands of the chiefs; and
4. Election and destoolment of chiefs had to be endorsed and supervised by the British.[5]

Although the British reduced the powers of the chiefs, the chiefs were protected by the Crown to ensure proper exercise of their duties. The chief's authority was challenged by the educated elite. This elite resented the judicial authority of the "illiterate chiefs." Lawyers were excluded from the Provincial Commissioners Courts where appeals from Native Tribunals were heard. On the other hand, the chief's position was fortified by the 1925 Guggisberg Constitution and the 1927 Native Administration Ordinance. For example, in the 1925 Constitution, six chiefs were elected by Provincial Councils established for the purpose of providing representation for the chiefs in the Legislative Council. They outnumbered the three members elected directly by the urban voters of Accra, Cape Coast, and Sekondi.[6] The Ashantis and the Northern Territory were also not represented in the Executive Council formed in 1925.[7]

It can be inferred from this that the majority of the Gold Coast people had little or no participation in national government. The 1946 Burns Constitution marked a turning point. For the first time, the Legislative Council became an African-dominated legislature. Out of the 30 members on the Legislative Council under the 1925 Constitution, nine were Africans; while under the Burns Constitution, 18 out of the 30 on the Legislative Council were Africans.[8] This was probably a driving force for the successful activities of the nationalist movements which occupied the politics of the Gold Coast in the 1940s and 1950s.

Economic Conditions

The colonial era (1844-1957) created a condition of economic dependence of the Gold Coast on the British.[9] There was insufficient effective demand for British manufactured goods in Britain due to low wages. Consequently, the British needed to find markets for their commodities overseas. Again, the British needed raw materials to keep their industries in operation. To achieve these ends, the British turned the Gold Coast into a monocultural economy and made cocoa the only major cash crop grown in the Gold Coast. Money received from cocoa sales was drained very quickly because of the exorbitant prices of the British manufactured goods. The Gold Coast was made a peripheral economy. The British avoided the integration of the Gold Coast economy into the world trading network. They encouraged the production of cocoa as a cash crop, and discouraged large production of foodstuffs.[10]

Not only was the Gold Coast not integrated into the world economy, its people were not allowed to own land that contained gold and other minerals. A prerequisite of capitalism is the establishment of land as private property. In the Gold Coast, the British settlers were the only people who could own the land that contained gold and other minerals, a practice which was contrary to the traditional land tenure system in which land (whether it contained minerals or not) was owned either by the tribes or families who held the rights in perpetuity. Again, the British had claim to all "waste" land (that is, unoccupied land). The British had two main reasons to be interested in the land. First, the British Crown doubted if enough cocoa will be produced without complete European takeover. They even planned on importing cheap Chinese labor to the Gold Coast to produce more cocoa.[11] The second, and probably more important reason, was to have complete control over the production of gold.[12]

The chiefs, the tribal groupings, and the educated elite resented the loss of their land rights. To protest this, the Aborigines Rights Protection Society (ARPS) was formed in the late nineteenth century. The ARPS sent a delegation in 1897 to London to protest the land bill. This protest was successful. By the end of 1897, the land bill died, leaving land in the hands of the Gold Coasters. The British were not happy about this and accordingly drafted a land bill in 1910 which gave the British the right to set up forest reserves, with two-fifths of any of the profits going to the owners and three-fifths kept by the government for administrative purposes.[13] Land ownership continued to be a source of controversy even shortly after Nkrumah assumed office.

In regard to infrastructural development, Governor Guggisberg's Ten-Year Development Plan (1920-1930) may be looked at as one directed towards the progress of the Gold Coast people. D.K. Greenstreet, however, argued that the plan was not only to improve the conditions of the Gold Coast people, but more importantly to improve trade.[14] The priorities of the plan indicate that Guggisberg attached greatest importance to improvements of communication networks which included harbors, railways, roads, telegraphs and telephones, and so forth. Out of the £24 million planned expenditure, £14 million (58 percent) was allotted to the development of railways, with £2 million and £1 million going into improvements in harbors and roads, respectively. Kodwo Ewusi further reported that about 72 percent was allotted to development of commmunciations.[15] Moreover, the 1951 Development Plan displayed communication as the largest single item constituting 35.3 percent of the total planned expenditure.[16] This trend of affairs leads Michael Crowder to point out that "if colonial powers can be said in any way to have brought an economic revolution in West Africa, it was through the construction of railways ... they were an immense stimulus to the production of the cash crops which they were designed to evacuate."[17]

In a survey quoted in the Seers and Ross report in 1950, it was found in a typical cocoa village that 32 percent of the population had malarial infection, 76 percent had ascana, 56 percent had hookworm, and 75 percent had active yaws.[18] This shows that a high proportion of Gold Coast citizens were ill from parasitic diseases. Only £1.79 million (7.3 percent) out of the £24 million planned expenditure was spent on water supply under the Guggisberg Ten-Year Development Plan.[19] One could say that not too much emphasis was laid on the health of the Gold Coasters, because the British were engrossed with their profits. One should, therefore, expect labor to be inefficient.

Similarly, the colonial government played only a small role in education. Under the Guggisberg Ten-Year Development Plan, only £1.1 million was allotted for the construction of schools and other public buildings which constituted only 4.5 percent of the planned expenditure, whereas for railways alone, £14.6 million (59.3 percent) was allotted. The major school project embarked upon was the building of The Prince of Wales College (now Achimota, where Nkrumah went to school) at a cost of £600,000[20]. Governor Guggisberg realized this problem and stated in his annual address in 1925 that the Gold Coast educational system was inadequate in size and had proved inefficient in its results because of its failure to emphasize and develop the character training of Gold Coast citizens. Total primary and middle school enrollment rose from 54,819 in 1930-1934 to 105,627 in 1940-1944.[21] The enrollment still accounted for only a small number of children relative to the total population. It may also be commented that while the increase in enrollment grew from year to year, the majority of children, especially the poor, could not afford the expenses involved. Moreover, those who could afford it did not get very good education, because the whole system of education was ineffective due to the government's unwillingness to increase very much the budget of education and Ghanaians had to rely on missionary schools.

The mining industry, however, was very well developed by the British. Between 1912 and 1931, the Ashanti Goldfields Corporation, the largest mining company in the country, produced two million ounces of gold at a total value of £8 million. And between 1935 and 1939, Gold Coast produced £558,000 worth of diamonds, and £790,000 worth of manganese.[22] The obvious conclusion that may be drawn from this is that the British were very interested in the development and the extraction of the resources that were going to benefit them directly. They needed the minerals and therefore they had more incentive to develop better ways of extracting them. Since education and health programs were not going to benefit them directly, they did not put much importance on them.

The external trade was favorable. It is reported that between 1912 and 1919, government revenue from external trade increased at an annual rate of 9 percent. The prosperity of the gold could also be inferred from the fact that Governor Guggisberg inherited a surplus of £1.2 million.[23] However, there were occasional swings of the external trade to the deficit side and back. For example, exports increased steadily from £1,340,000 in 1904 to £5,425,000 in 1913. Exports for 1920 reached a peak of £12,352,000; dropped to £6,942,000 in 1921, and went back up to £12,104,000 in 1926.[24] The swings could be attributed to the disastrous effect of the fall in cocoa prices. One may question why then the Gold Coast was underdeveloped. The answer may be that although the Gold Coast was making the money, the British overlords did not spend the money in programs that were going to develop the Gold Coast. (The discussion of Guggisberg's Ten-Year Development Plan clarifies this point.) Also, the British directed the money received from cocoa sales to develop the metropolitan economy, leaving the Gold Coast backward. The foregoing discussion of the political, economic, and social conditions formed the background against which Nkrumah became president in 1957 after leading the Gold Coast to independence from the British.

The Life and Career of Nkrumah

Kwame Nkrumah was the first and only child of his mother. Although there were controversies as to what his actual date of birth was, his mother confirmed that he was born somewhere in the middle of September, 1909, at Nkroful, a southern village. And since his first name "Kwame" is the first name of all males from his region born on Saturday, the date seemed to be

September 18, 1909.[25] This uncertainty is an undoubted manifestation of the high illiteracy level of the Gold Coast citizens at the time of Nkrumah's birth. Nkrumah wrote in his autobiography that his mother had told him she thought he was dead since it took him so long to show signs of life at the time of his birth.[26] This incident would make people think that Nkrumah was a weak infant. One of the traditions of the Akan ethnic group, to which Nkrumah belonged, was that the first born is always less bright than average. So, for Nkrumah, to be the first born child implied that he would not be highly intelligent. Nkrumah's father, a goldsmith, was described as a man of very strong character which probably had some impact on Nkrumah later on. It is written that Nkrumah's father was poor and could not afford to give Nkrumah even toys to play with. Since polygamy was the tradition, Nkrumah had several half brothers and half sisters. Unlike other children who feared ghosts, Nkrumah did not and even wished to be one.[27] This longing may be psychologically significant, but the conclusion that he possessed psychic powers is questionable. At the age of six, Nkrumah went to school, which he did not like initially. Born to a poor family, he started raising chickens to help pay for his school expenses. Nkrumah was a Catholic, like his mother, although his father did not go to church.[28]

After graduation from the elementary school, when he was 17, Nkrumah became a pupil teacher for one year at Half Assini. In 1926, the principal of Achimota College visited Nkrumah's school and became impressed with how he taught standing on a box because of his height. The principal recommended him to go to his college (Achimota College) in which Nkrumah enrolled the following year. It was at Achimota College that Nkrumah's nationalism was first aroused. He was influenced by the vice president of Achimota College, Dr. Kwegir Aggrey, the first Ghanaian member of the staff, whose principles of equality and togetherness attracted him. Aggrey was a good orator. Nkrumah quoted Aggrey to have once said, "You can play a tune of sorts on the white keys, and you can play a tune of sorts on the black keys, but for harmony you must use both the black and white."[29] Like Aggrey, Nkrumah was against racism and believed that for a better world blacks and whites should work together. When Aggrey went on vacation in New York, he died there. This discouraged Nkrumah because Aggrey's presence was quite a guiding light to him. Nkrumah was made the school prefect during which period he became very interested in public speaking. He formed a debating society which was a forum for speech-making. Nkrumah always won his debates, showing that he was an articulate and convincing orator. He graduated in 1930 and taught in primary school for five years, after which he decided to go to school in the United States.[30]

His decision to pursue his studies in the U.S. is made clear in his words,

In all things, I have held myself to but one ambition, and that is, to make necessary arrangements to continue my education in a university of the United States of America, that I may be better prepared, and still be of better use to my fellow men ... and I am forced to conclude with the same words; so much to do, so little done.[31]

Although Lincoln University in Pennsylvania gave him a scholarship, his savings were not enough to pay for his voyage, so he went to a relative who was staying in Nigeria for help. He finally got enough money to get a third-class ticket from Takoradi to London to get the American visa, since there was no American consul in the Gold Coast.

Nkrumah arrived in the U.S. in 1935. His life in the U.S. was quite unbearable for him. He was not only a student, but a worker as well in order to meet other expenses. He worked at a soap factory at Harlem, where he had to collect animal fat into a wheelbarrow to be transported to the main plant. He also worked as a steward in a ship sailing between New York and Mexico.[32] His income was not even enough for lodging, so he rode the subway for a nickel until the night passed.[33] This may seem a little exaggerated, but it still brings out the fact that Nkrumah came from a poor background and so he had to be self-supporting.

At Lincoln University, Nkrumah helped to organize the African Students' Association of America and Canada and founded the *African Interpreter* as their newspaper. The purpose of the association was to provide a common ground for Africans and Black Americans to work together for liberation and freedom. He received a bachelor's degree in Sociology and Economics from Lincoln University in Pennsylvania in 1939. He had planned to go to the Columbia University School of Journalism, but because of financial difficulties, he had to accept an offer to teach Philosophy at Lincoln University. In 1943, he received the Master of Arts degree in Philosophy from the University of Pennsylvania. He finished the courses and preliminary examinations in two years for the Doctor of Philosophy degree from the University of Pennsylvania; what was left was the thesis. Again, he had to quit school and work to make ends meet. In May, 1945, he left New York for London.[34]

Nkrumah went to London with his first draft of *Towards Colonial Freedom*, in which he emphasized his commitment to anti-colonial struggle. He became involved in the Pan African Congress, whose objective was to bring about concerted effort among Africans, West Indians, and Black Americans in their struggle for freedom and justice and condemnation of capitalism. At the Fifth Pan African Congress in Manchester in 1945, Nkrumah's African political consciousness was reawakened. It is reported that the Congress adopted socialist ideology, so it was no surprise for Nkrumah to resort to socialism. The participants in the meeting included such dignitaries as W.E.B. DuBois and Dr. Peter Milliard, who was one of the founders of the National Association for the Advancement of Colored People (NAACP). They all asserted the necessity of organized political machinery as important for the final overthrow of colonialism. In setting up a working committee for this objective, Nkrumah was appointed the General Secretary. In England, Nkrumah also experienced racism, although he admitted that it was not as severe as in the U.S.[35] Generally, Nkrumah did not look at the problem in terms of color, but in terms of capitalist exploitation and the class struggle. To fight capitalism, he formed an organization called The Circle which had the objective of relentlessly fighting foreign domination and exploitation. Its philosophy was ''scientific socialism'' which has been discussed in Chapter 2. Moreover, Nkrumah was a member of the West African National Secretariat, whose motto was ''For unity and absolute independence.'' And in 1945, they published the newspaper *The New African*.[36] Nkrumah's involvement in the West African National Secretariat influenced his goal of struggle and became one who would settle for nothing short of complete independence.

During his London days, he was against the subservient approach of non-violence. He is known to have said that ''independence cannot come through delegations, gifts, charity, paternalism, grants, concessions, proclamations, charters, or reformism.''[37] After completing his law degree at London School of Economics in 1947, he left for the Gold Coast.[38]

Nkrumah's Rise to Power

This section of the study will deal with the political activities of Nkrumah from the time of his return from London in 1947 until he became president in 1957. At this juncture, a brief survey of the major political parties in the Gold Coast is in order.

The United Gold Coast Convention (UGCC)

This was the first political organization to talk in practical terms of self-government, which it declared should be achieved in the shortest possible time. It was formed in August, 1947, by a small group of southern lawyers and businessmen. The leader was Dr. J. B. Danquah and its General Secretary was Nkrumah who returned from London specifically to take the appointment. Nkrumah defected and formed the Convention Peoples Party (CPP). The UGCC contested and was defeated in the 1951 general elections and was, therefore, dissolved the following year.[39]

Convention People's Party (CPP)

This was the main nationalist party, formed in June, 1949, by Nkrumah as a militant breakaway movement from the UGCC. It drew most of its support from the commoners, regardless of their ethnic backgrounds. It demanded "self-government *now*" and successfully contested and won the 1951, 1954, and 1956 elections.[40] (Nkrumah's ideas for the party and its organization are discussed in Chapter 2.)

National Liberation Movement (NLM)

This political organization was formed in 1954. Most of its members were Ashantis (a people who lived in the central part of Ghana and who were the largest ethnic group). It demanded the revival of the Ashanti Legendry and also demanded powers the kings had lost. Moreover, it demanded federation among all the ethnic groups. It was the strongest opposition party to the CPP. It contested and lost the 1956 elections and faded away.[41]

United Party (UP)

Formed in 1957, the UP was composed of all the opposition parties to the CPP who lost the 1956 elections. They included the Northern Peoples' Party (a northern-based party formed in 1954 with its largest support drawn from chiefs), and the Muslim Association Party (formed by a majority of Muslim communities which numbered approximately 6.5 percent of the population).[42]

Having introduced these political organizations, we can now discuss Nkrumah's rise to power.

Nkrumah returned to the Gold Coast in 1947 at the invitation of the UGCC, the only organized nationalist movement in the Gold Coast, to become their General Secretary.[43] The UGCC embarked upon constant demonstrations in their struggle for independence.[44] However, reports show that Nkrumah found the UGCC to be too conservative and too slow in their search for independence. Consequently, he formed his own party, the CPP, in June, 1949. Contrary to the slow approach adopted by the UGCC, Nkrumah wanted independence "now," which made his approach more militant.[45] The six-point program of the CPP included the following:

1. To fight by all constitutional means for the achievement of self-government;
2. To serve as a vigorous political vanguard with the aim of eradicating oppression and establishing democratic rule;
3. To work towards the unity of the chiefs and people of all the Gold Coast territories;
4. To work in the country to improve employment conditions;
5. To work for the construction of the country; and
6. To work towards the unity and independence of all African states.[46]

From the foregoing discussion, it has been made clear that all the political organizations had the objective of leading the Gold Coast to independence. However,, their approaches differed in the sense that while the UGCC and the other parties approved independence at the earliest possible time, Nkrumah and his CPP wanted independence immediately. I believe that Nkrumah's charismatic appeal was the most important attribute which drew him the largest following. For this reason, Nkrumah's rise to power will be analyzed in the light of his charismatic appeal. What made Nkrumah and the CPP more acceptable in the Gold Coast (later Ghana) than the other political organizations? The answer is simply his charisma.

In addressing the relevance of Max Weber's analysis to Nkrumah's situation at this point, two general observations can be made. According to Weber's theory, charismatic leaders emerge "in time of psychic, physical, economic, ethical, religious, and political distress" and also charisma inspires its followers with "a devotion born of distress and enthusiasm."[47] Dankwart A. Rustow supported Weber when he wrote that charismatic leadership emerges during crisis situations.[48] Nkrumah emerged at a time when the Gold Coast people were in a crisis and fighting for independence. So one can argue that Weber's theory can be applied to Nkrumah. Secondly, Weber's thesis points out that charismatic leaders usually tend to be innovative and revolutionary in character. They fight for new ways by rejecting the old ones.[49] Reinhard Bendix makes the same point. To Bendix, "The charismatic leader is always a radical who challenges established practice by going to the root of the matter."[50] The objectives of the CPP illustrate this point.[51] Nkrumah was unhappy about the presence of the British and relentlessly struggled to change that status quo by achieving independence. It must also be said that only few African leaders operating in similar circumstances were charismatic. This means that there were other factors present in Nkrumah's situation which were absent in other African countries. For example, Nkrumah embarked on and successfully achieved independence for Ghana which no other black African country had previously done. This undoubtedly contributed greatly to the invocation of Nkrumah's charismatic appeal.

David Apter points out that charismatic leaders tend to be those who spearhead the independence of the country in question.[52] This same idea has been emphasized by Willner.[53] The motion calling for independence was moved by Nkrumah in the Legislative Assembly of August 3, 1956. This made independence possible on March 6, 1957.[54]

W.G. Runciman, however, argued that the CPP was a revolutionary party only in a limited sense of the term. He wrote that power was peacefully handed over by the colonial government. To him, Nkrumah only speeded up the handover.[55] Be that as it may, the fact that Nkrumah made some difference is significant. Edward Shils believed that the ability of the charismatic leader to attract a popular following is critical to facilitate this kind of transition.[56] During Nkrumah's charismatic leadership he could attract crowds.[57] A diverse following joined him, including journalists, teachers, ex-servicemen, small-scale businessmen, and many others parts of the population.[58] It is also suggested that the CPP had better local organization and patronage and that this accounted for the larger following.[59] Runciman questions the reliance of better organization as the cause of large following. Instead, he wrote that because of the competition between the nationalist parties, charismatic leaders tend to make more spectacular promises than their rivals; and that it is the massive promises which give them the appeal.[60]

Although this idea seems accurate to Willner, she also argues that the only way legitimacy will remain charismatic depends upon the leader's ability to ensure continuous successes.[61]

The nature of the opposition posed no threats to Nkrumah's larger following. Although there were opposition parties like the NLM, NPP, and UP, this was not a danger to CPP leadership. In the Gold Coasts's situation, differences of opinion on national issues were very marginal between the parties. For example, the CPP, NLM, and NPP all had the twin aims of political independence and economic development. Moreover, no significant class differences in terms of support for the parties existed within the population. The UP and NLM were all regional movements centered on traditional authorities. For instance, the NLM wanted retention of traditional powers which used to be exercised by the chiefs. This was not a program which could have the characteristics of a mass national party. Moreover, there were few ideological differences–all the parties favored socialism. In this situation, W. B. Birmingham wrote that the first party to capture power and lead is likely to capture and retain charismatic legitimacy. The CPP was the first party to do this. Not surprisingly, therefore, Nkrumah was able to reinforce this opportunity with his better organizational strategy and propaganda.[62]

Supporting Birmingham, Dennis Austin added that kinship ties were the only effective inducement to voters to support the opposition. Since CPP was supported by a vast majority of the population, the ethnic support given to the NLM, NPP, and UP could not affect the CPP and Nkrumah's victory.[63] The ethnic groups included the Akan, Ewe, Ga, Dagomba, and Nzima. When Nkrumah broke away from the UGCC. Nkrumah's opponents attempted to discredit him in the eyes of the Ga ethnic group by repeatedly referring to his Nzimah ethnic group origin but they were not successful as his victories in the 1951, 1954, and 1956 election results indicated.[64]

It has been asserted that nearly all political charismatic leaders have also been described as possessing oratorical skills.[65] Nkrumah is described as a very good orator and possessing a good sense of the symbolic power of language.[66] His power of language was an advantage to his party to win the elections in 1951, 1954, and 1956. Nkrumah was also a person who was unwilling to accept failure. He radiated a buoyant confidence in the rightness of his activities. Even in moments of discouragement and difficulty,

Nkrumah displayed stubborn confidence, all of which are characteristics of charismatic leaders.[67] Nkrumah is described by Bankhole Timothy, a biographer, as able to remain calm during crisis situations and make jokes during difficulties.[68]

During his campaigning, Nkrumah propounded ideas so concrete to imply that all the plagues of the Gold Coast would come to an abrupt end if the people cooperated with him to bring about the end of colonial rule.[69] This notion of having a peculiar sense of mission was present in Nkrumah which undoubtedly contributed to his charismatic appeal and political success.

Max Weber postulated that charismatic leaders tend to be sensitive and responsive to the dominant culture.[70] Nkrumah's political rivals, like J. B. Danquah of the UGCC, believed in reconstructing the Gold Coast according to Western standards. They were, therefore, unwilling to shape the UGCC incorporating the aspirations of the people. Nkrumah, on the other hand, followed a different course and made it known to the people the need to incorporate their aspirations for a better social and economic change.[71] Moreover, while Nkrumah agitated for "positive action" as a style to be followed to achieve independence,[72] his political rivals, the UGCC, wanted independence to be given at the time the British deemed proper. Positive action was a non-conspiratorial strategy to achieve independence. By this strategy, Nkrumah recommended such weapons as strikes, boycotts, and non-cooperation based on the principle of non-violence.[73] The "positive action" was eventually changed to "tactical action" which was a compromising approach to achieve independence.[74] Nkrumah even attributed the 1954 constitutional reforms as the effect of the "tactical action" plan in which the CPP won 79 out of the 104 seats.[75] No matter how we may interpret Nkrumah's strategy, the difference in style still remains when compared to his opponents. For example, the UGCC followed rules and conditions laid down by the colonial rulers because the UGCC feared mass political awakening. On the other hand, Nkrumah believed in mass mobilization and also inculcated into his followers a sense of political awareness.[76]

It has been pointed out that one of the characteristics of charismatic leaders is their ability to initiate and maintain correspondence with the voters and shape their lifestyle with the people.[77] It is reported that the masses knew Nkrumah more than his opponents. He often stayed in the huts of villagers and ate with them. The masses, therefore, believed that he had deep concern for the common man.[78] This accounted partly for CPP's victories in the 1951, 1954, and 1956 elections.

Nkrumah's interest in women was clearly demonstrated during his political rallies. Willner believed that charismatic leaders are lovers of women.[79] Nkrumah is quoted to have said to some women at one of his political rallies, "You are all my brides."[80] Nkrumah married early, and also he had several children by various mistresses. He ended up marrying an Egyptian woman, Madame Fathia.[81] She was the daughter of another charismatic leader, Gamal Abdul Nasser of Egypt.

Another advantage Nkrumah enjoyed over his political rivals was that he had a good sense of personal drama and role during his campaigning and even thereafter. Ghanaians gave him the African appellation "show boy," meaning that he was not only dramatic, but also he had in him something of the small child. This implied that he lacked maturity and showed his ever preparedness to share his achievements with others and also tried to make people pleased at his success just like children do.[82] Moreover, in pursuit of his "show boy" principle, he made the youth part and parcel of his CPP. Nkrumah believed that for socialism to be constructed, socialists are needed. He found the answer in the youth and, therefore, formed the Committee on Youth Organization (CYO) as a machinery for mobilizing the youth.[83] With the youth firmly behind him as well as the mass support, victory was inevitable.

Dankwart A. Rustow believed that one of the charismatic invocations is the ability to maintain a high energy level.[84] Bankhole Timothy credited Nkrumah with his ability to live on a minimum of sleep as well as food.[85] If Nkrumah exhibited a high level of vitality, then it would make sense to expect people to think of him as superhuman. Whether charismatic leaders have this vitality is unclear. It is probable that they get tired, but are able to make invisible any signs of exhaustion.[86] Susanne Hoeber Rudolph reported that the assistants who accompanied Nkrumah on his trips bear testimony that he had an untiring energy level.[87] This was definitely to Nkrumah's advantage, for his followers exaggerated and developed a myth about his "untiring dedication to work and unflagging vitality."[88] And, if people were going to vote for someone to work for a change, it was likely for Nkrumah to be elected because of this myth of extraordinary degree of vitality.

There was a general election in 1951 and CPP won 33 out of the 38 seats.

In the 1951 plebiscite, Nkrumah was elected for Accra Central Region with 22,780 votes out of 23,122 which was the largest individual poll so far recorded. Nkrumah was by then in prison for leading demonstrations against colonial rule. And being the leader of the CPP, he was released and was appointed Leader of Government Business.[89]   Moreover, elections were held in 1954 and 1956 which the CPP won. In the 1954 elections, CPP won 72 seats out of 104 seats by polling 391, 817 votes, while the Independents received 156,401 and the Ghana People's Congress (GPC), which Britain supported, won only one seat with a total of 32,168.[90]   When an election was held in 1956, the CPP won 71 seats and the NLM only 12. See Table 1 for a complete summary of the 1956 elections.

One may question whether Nkrumah achieved charismatic following before or after being in power. Willner clearly distinguishes preaccession and postaccession generation of charismatic relationship.[91] In Nkrumah's case, it becomes difficult to put him in one particular group. For example, Nkrumah was rhetorical, omniscient and was revolutionary, all of which helped to generate his charismatic effect over wider radius as well as popularity. His preaccession charisma became more broadly diffused after obtaining office which can be referred to as his postaccession charismatic era.

It can, therefore, be asserted that Nkrumah had charisma even before he came into power, and with the power given, he was able to magnify the appeal. Furthermore, David Apter argues that when a leader's personality is genuinely charismatic, his charisma will begin to show even before he becomes politically powerful.[92] The following chapter will analyze Nkrumah's implementation of his programs in his effort to develop Ghana.

Table 1
1956 Election Results

	Colony		TVT		Ashanti		North		Total		% of Total Votes Cast
	Seats	Votes	Seats	Votes	Seats	Votes	Seats	Votes	Seats	Votes	
Convention People's Party	44	179,024	8	55,508	8	96,968	11	66,641	71	398,141	57
Non-Convention People's Party	0	42,602	5	46,076	13	127,601	15	82,837	33	299,116	43
National Liberation Movement	0	26,124	--	--	12	119,533	--	--	12	145,657	
Moslem Association Party	0	1,814	--	--	1	7,565	0	1,732	1	11,111	
Northern People's Party	--	--	--	--	--	--	15	72,440	15	72,440	
Togoland Congress	--	--	2	20,352	--	--	--	--	2	20,352	
Federated Youth Organization	0	1,230	1	5,617	--	--	--	--	1	6,847	
Wassaw Youth Association	0	3,898	--	--	--	--	--	--	0	3,898	
Independents	0	9,536	2	20,107	0	503	0	8,665	2	38,811	
	44	221,626	13	101,584	21	224,569	26	149,478	104	697,257	100

Source: Dennis Austin, *Politics in Ghana, 1946-1960* (London: Oxford University Press, 1970), p. 354

Note: The Independents include Rev. F.R. Amatowobla in support of the Togoland Congress, and B. A. Konu who later joined the CPP. The five unopposed seats have been added to the CPP total.

Endnotes

[1] Irving Kaplan, James L. McLaughlin et al., *Area Handbook for Ghana* (Washington, D.C.; U.S. Government Printing Office, 1971), pp.87-102.

[2] Thomas A. Howell and Jeffrey P. Rajasooria, *Ghana and Nkrumah* (New York: Facts on Files, Inc., 1972), pp. 2-5.

[3] Michael Crowder, *West Africa Under Colonial Rule* (Evanston: Northwestern university Press, 1968), p. 165.

[4] David E. Apter, *Ghana in Transition,* 2nd ed. (Princeton: Princeton University Press, 1972), p. 20.

[5] Ibid. "Destoolment" is particular to the Ashanti ethnic group of Ghana. The idea of the stool dates back to the mid-17th century when Okomfo Anokye, a powerful fetish priest, caught a "Golden Stool" from the sky. Anokye gave the stool to the then Ashanti king, Nana Osei Tutu. The stool became the spiritual embodiment of the Ashantis with the king as the sole custodian. From that time on, any new chief chosen was to have automatic access to the stool. Thus, he was "enstooled." Also when a chief abused his power, he was unseated and this was referred to as "destoolment," meaning that the chief was no longer the spiritual leader of the people. Hence, the word "destoolment."

[6] Ibid.

[7] Crowder, *West Africa Under Colonial Rule,* pp. 222-224.

[8] Apter, *Ghana in Transition,* pp. 136, 142-143.

[9] Rhoda Howard, *Colonialism and Underdevelopment in Ghana* (New York: African Publishing Company, 1978), p. 22; Richard Harris, *The Political Economy of Africa* (New York: John Wiley and Sons, 1975), p. 52 and Ian Roxborough, *Theories of Underdevelopment* (London: Macmillan Press Ltd., 1979), p. 55.

[10] Howard, *Colonialism and Underdevelopment in Ghana,* pp. 19-21.

[11] Ibid., pp. 37-39.

[12] Ibid.

[13] Ibid., pp. 39-44.

[14] D.K. Greenstreet, "The Guggisberg Ten-Year Development Plan," *The Economic Bulletin of Ghana,* 8(1), (1964), p. 21.

[15] Kodwo Ewusi, *Economic Development Planning in Ghana* (New York: Exposition Press, 1973), pp. 19-21.

[16] Ibid., p. 24.

[17] Crowder, *West Africa Under Colonial Rule*, p. 276.

[18] Apter, *Ghana in Transition,* p. 65.

[19] Ewusi, *Economic Development Planning in Ghana,* p. 20.

[20] Ibid.

[21] G. B. Kay and Stephen Hymer, *The Political Economy of Colonialism in Ghana* (Cambridge: Cambridge University Press, 1972), p. 407 and *Kwame Nkrumah* (London: Panaf, 1974), p. 96. It reported the literacy rate of Ghana in 1966 as 16.3 percent as opposed to 5.7 percent literacy rate in Nigeria.

[22] Kay and Hymer, *The Political Economy of Colonialism in Ghana,* p. 325; and Howard, *Colonialism and Underdevelopment in Ghana,* p. 61.

[23] Ewusi, *Economic Development Planning in Ghana,* pp. 21-22.

[24] Kay and Hymer, *The Political Economy of Colonialism in Ghana,* pp. 325-326.

[25] *Kwame Nkrumah,* p. 17; and Kwame Nkrumah, *The Autobiography of Kwame Nkrumah* (New York: Thomas Nelson and Sons, 1957), p. 5.

[26] Nkrumah, *The Autobiography of Kwame Nkrumah,* p. 6.

[27] Ibid., pp. 6-14.

[28] Ibid., p. 12.

[29] Ibid., p. 16.

[30] Ibid., p. 17-22.

[31] Ibid., p. 20.

[32] *Kwame Nkrumah,* p. 20.

[33] Ibid., p. 22.

[34] Ibid., pp. 22-34.

[35] Ibid., p. 29-33.

[36] Ibid.

[37] Kwame Nkrumah, *Towards Colonial Freedom* (New York: International Publishers, 1793), p. xviii.

[38] *Kwame Nkrumah,* p. 35.

[39] George Padmore, *The Gold Coast Revolution* (London: Dennis Dobson Ltd., 1963), pp. 60-62, 68.

[40] Ibid., pp. 67-71.

[41] Basil Davidson, *Black Star: A View of the Life and Times of Nkrumah* (London: Clark and Brendon, Ltd., 1973), pp. 146-151, 167-168.

[42] Dennis Austin, *Politics in Ghana, 1946-1960* (London: Oxford University Press, 1970), pp. 384-386.

[43] *Kwame Nkrumah*, p. 35.

[44] Ibid., p. 37.

[45] Howell and Rajasooria, *Ghana and Nkrumah*, p. 10

[46] Nkrumah, *The Autobiography of Kwame Nkrumah*, p. 101

[47] Hans Gerth and C. Mills, eds., *From Max Weber: Essays in Sociology* (New York: Oxford University Press, 1946), pp. 245, 249. They speak of charismatic leaders as self-appointed leaders who are followed by those who are in distress and who need to follow the leader because they believe him to be extraordinarily qualified to solve their problems.

[48] Dankwart A. Rustow, "Ataturk as Founder of a State," *Daedalus*, 97 (Summer 1968), p. 794; and Ann Ruth Willner, *Charismatic Political Leadership* (Princeton: Princeton University Press, 1968), p. 8.

[49] Max Weber, ed., *The Theory of Social and Economic Organization* (New York: The Free Press, 1947), pp. 214, 362-363.

[50] Reinhard Bendix, *Max Weber: An Intellectual Portrait* (London: Methuen, 1966), p. 300.

[51] *Kwame Nkrumah*, p. 45.

[52] David E. Apter, *Ghana in Transition*, 1st ed. (New York: Atheneum, 1963), pp. 320-330.

[53] Ann Ruth Willner and Dorothy Willner, "The Rise and Role of Charismatic Leaders," *The Annals of the American Academy of Political and Social Science*, 358 (March 1965), pp. 77-78. The Willners wrote: "Charismatic leadership seems to flourish today particularly in the newer states that were formerly under colonial rule" (p. 80).

[54] Howell and Rajasooria, *Ghana and Nkrumah*, pp. 27-30.

[55] W.G. Runciman, "Charismatic Legitimacy and One-Party Rule in Ghana," *European Journal of Sociology*, 4 (1963), p. 154.

[56] Edward Shils, "The Concentration and Dispersion of Charisma," *World Politics*, 11 (October 1958), pp. 1-19.

57 David Apter, "Nkrumah, Charisma and the Coup," *Daedalus,* 97 (Summer 1968), p. 767.

58 Ibid., p. 768.

59 Ibid., pp. 739, 767.

60 Runciman, "Charismatic Legitimacy and One-Party Rule in Ghana," p. 158.

61 Willner, *Charismatic Political Leadership,* p. 9.

62 W.B. Birmingham and G. Jahoda, "A Pre-election Survey in a Semi-literate Society," *Public Opinion Quarterly,* 19 (1955), p. 152.

63 Dennis Austin, "Elections in an African Rural Area," *Africa,* 21 (1961), pp. 1-18.

64 Nkrumah, *The Autobiography of Kwame Nkrumah,* p. 105.

65 Willner, *Charismatic Political Leadership,* p. 103; and *Kwame Nkrumah,* p. 42.

66 Apter, "Nkrumah, Charisma and the Coup," p. 774.

67 Ibid., p. 749.

68 Bankhole Timothy, *Kwame Nkrumah: His Rise to Power* (Evanston: Northwestern University Press, 1961), p. 169.

69 *Kwame Nkrumah,* p. 61.

70 Weber, *The Theory of Social and Economic Organization,* pp. 71, 363.

71 *Kwame Nkrumah,* p. 41.

72 Padmore, *The Gold Coast Revolution,* pp. 79-80.

73 Patrick Dunkan, "Non-Violence at Accra," *Africa Today,* 6 (1959), pp. 30-33; Padmore, *The Gold Coast Revolution,* p. 80.

74 Runciman, "Charismatic Legitimacy and One-Party Rule in Ghana," p. 156.

75 Ibid.

76 *Kwame Nkrumah,* p. 41.

77 Willner, *Charismatic Political Leadership,* p. 67.

78 *Kwame Nkrumah,* pp. 44-45; and Willner, *Charismatic Political Leadership,* p. 67.

[79] Willner, *Charismatic Political Leadership,* p. 69.

[80] Richard Wright, *Black Power* (New York: Harper, 1954).

[81] Apter, "Nkrumah, Charisma and the Coup," p. 775.

[82] Ibid.

[83] *Kwame Nkrumah,* p. 79.

[84] Rustow, "Atatürk as Founder of a State," p. 794.

[85] Timothy, *Kwame Nkrumah: His Rise to Power,* p. 168

[86] Robert J. Alexander, *Prophets of the Revolution* (New York: Macmillan Company, 1962), pp. 278-279.

[87] Susanne Hoeber Rudolph, "The New Courage: An Essay on Gandhi's Psychology," *World Politics,* 16 (October 1693), p. 107.

[88] Willner, *Charismatic Political Leadership,* p. 63.

[89] *Kwame Nkrumah,* pp. 62, 70.

[90] Austin, *Politics in Ghana, 1946-1960,* p. 354.

[91] Willner, *Charismatic Political Leadership,* p. 14.

[92] Apter, "Nkrumah, Charisma and the Coup," p. 740.

Discussion Questions

1. Why did the British adopt the "indirect rule" system in their African colonial territories?

2. Carefully trace Nkrumah's early life to his rise to power. Can we engage in a psychoanalysis of his life and career?

Chapter 4
Implementation

This chapter examines Nkrumah's response to Ghanaian under-development. His theoretical approaches to the problem of Ghanaian development will be analyzed and, in each case, some determination will be made as to the practicality of those ideas. The themes to be examined are all expressions of Nkrumah's socialism. Nkrumah took a socialist approach for Ghanaian development. And he also took a socialist outlook for international matters.

Thus, the chapter will be divided into three major sections. The first section will examine Nkrumah's domestic policies in terms of four key substantive dimensions:

1. State administration and government
2. Industrialization policies
3. Agricultural policies, and
4. Social policies (education and health).

Secondly, we will analyze Nkrumah's foreign policy. This will be divided into two broad sections:

1. His policy in Africa, and
2. His policy outside Africa.

The third major category will be devoted to the evaluation of Nkrumah's regime performance.

Domestic Policy

Nkrumah favored a socialist strategy for Ghana's development. Thus, most of his internal programs in Ghana were expressions of his socialism. Before getting into the discussion of his specific socialist policies, I will first examine his notion of the state and how he organized it administratively to take on the various socialist programs.

Administration and Government

Socialism, the 1962 document "A Programme for Work and Happiness" announced, "can be achieved only by a rapid change in the socioeconomic structure of the country ... it is absolutely necessary to have strong ... and highly centralized government."[1] This meant that power had to be concentrated in the country's leadership. In fact, by 1962 very considerable power indeed was concentrated in the President's Office which controlled almost every aspect of economic planning, general policy, and foreign policy, together with control of the armed forces and the Civil Service.[2]

Administrative dualism existed in Nkrumah's administration. The Central Administration was composed of the Office of the President and the Ministries and Departments with each having its own operational procedures. The central administrative apparatus was organized into 10 ministries. Each ministry contained departments which dealt with largely complementary subjects. For example, under the Ministry of Education were departments which dealt with formal and informal education as well as reform and rehabilitation of prisoners. While the latter (ministries and departments) were composed to operate in accordance with such bureaucratic values as consistency and fairness in rule application, the operations of the former (Office of the President) were dominated by considerations of political necessity.[3] Indeed, on occasion, as the Principal Secretary of the Ministry of Communications observed in 1965, the ministries and departments had to dispense with their bureaucratic procedures.[4] Thus, these institutions discarded their conventional operational methods at the behest of the president.

Prior to the 1960 Constitution, the ministers were under constant pressures from the National Assembly Public Accounts Committee and the Auditor-General's Department to comply with financial and administrative instructions. This made it somewhat difficult for Nkrumah to get his way quickly. Nkrumah found a solution to this in the 1960 Republican Constitution. Under the 1960 Republican Constitution, the president was empowered to expand the presidential office. Nkrumah, accordingly, expanded the presidential sector and the presidential sector took over from the ministerial sector all the political aspects of its functions.[5] As a result, the Office of the President became responsible for determining national objectives, priorities, strategies and allocation of resources. The ministries and the departments were restricted to the implementation, not the formulation, of policies and the management of programs.

At the regional level, the CPP played a vital role. Political appointees were made regional representatives of the central government. The political appointees, Regional Commissioners (RCs), were charged with regional administrative responsibilities. There were also regional branches of the ministries and departments, but they were made subordinate to the RCs.[6] Thus, the choice of political appointees as the most authoritative figures in regional administration marked a concrete attempt to infuse the dynamism of the CPP control and leadership into regional administration.

At the local level too, the CPP appointed politicians as the District Commissioners (DCs) who were in charge of administration at the local level. The DCs reported to the RCs who then reported to the Office of the President.

The DCs had no powers over chieftaincy matters, the Chieftaincy Secretariat of the Office of the President was in charge of chieftaincy matters.[7]

From the above discussion, it is clear that Nkrumah faced opposition from a) the chiefs and also b) the bureaucrats whose powers had been taken away from them.

The Chiefs. In the most part, the citizens of newly independent states are still in the grip of their traditional institutions. They are, therefore, unwilling to accept a new loyalty, without hesitation, if the new loyalty is not parallel to the epoch of the traditional principles.[8] As a strategy for centralizing power to be strictly exercised by centralized state control, Nkrumah made attempts to undercut the significance of the powers enjoyed by the traditional chiefs before and during the indirect rule system.

By the 1960 Chieftaincy Act, Nkrumah reduced the chiefs' status to that of stipendiary of the central government, dependent in fact for office or official recognition, on the CPP government. Also, the chiefs were required to perform specific functions in accordance with the statutes laid down by the CPP government.[9] For example, the Chieftaincy Secretariat of the Office of the President was in charge of chieftaincy affairs, and this is a role the chiefs were performing prior to the CPP administration. Thus, the chiefs were no longer going to play a significant role in the social, political, or governmental life of the country. The power to enstool and destool was given to the Ministry of Local Government.[10]

For Nkrumah to deny the chiefs their right to exercise their authority in the context of the new political institutions appeared to the chiefs that the new order had come to supplant the old, but not to co-exist.[11] Unquestionably, the traditional sector was a continuous source of opposition against Nkrumah and the CPP.

For a charismatic legitimacy to be strong, the leader must have a due respect and recognition of the culture and tradition within which he or she is operating. For Nkrumah to alienate the chiefs meant separating the traditional from modern politics, which tended to contradict the claim to charismatic invocation in Weberian terms. Claude Ake writes that political institutional change is fundamentally disruptive of traditional institutions for the transition requires either a modification or abandonment of the indigenous sociocultural system.[12] David Apter agrees with this proposition and adds that the new leader, therefore, becomes the nucleus of unity.[13] This new leader was, therefore, able to hold together those whom the slackening bonds of tradition have left with no common identity. Furthermore, tribal or ethnic differences could be minimized with the emergence of a charismatic leader who looked at all the people as citizens of the country, rather than according to their ethnic origins.

These authors seem confused about Nkrumah's relationship with the chiefs. In fact, Nkrumah respected tradition insofar as it did not interfere with the actions he considered necessary to create a modern state. Since tribalism has been a major drawback in the colonial era as a result of its divisive tendencies, Nkrumah believed in national reconstruction based on national unity and solidarity other than on tribal ties. And, regardless of one's ethnic origin, Nkrumah attempted to raise the standard of living and welfare of all Ghanaian citizens (not as Ashantis, Fantis, Ewes, or Gas). The fact that Dr. Limann in 1979 became the president of Ghana is an important contribution of Nkrumah in the solution of the tribal problems in Ghana. (Limann comes from the Ntafo tribe in the north which had been considered the most inferior tribe in Ghana. The North was the most backward at the time and consequently would not be expected to be an important contributor to the country. The Ntafos are mostly used on the farms as laborers by the other ethnic groups.)

The Bureaucracy. According to Max Weber, charismatic authority is essentially irrational in the sense that it has no recognition of rules. Bureaucratic authority is bound by intellectually analyzable rules.[14] So it may be inferred that where charismatic authority exists, bureaucracy is restricted to implementation and no bureaucratic leadership. Not surprisingly, Nkrumah wrote that the Ghanaian bureaucratic bourgeoisie acted as a brake on socialist policies.[15] Nevertheless, one cannot blame Nkrumah for the bureaucratic inefficiency, because the bureaucracy had its problem of inefficiency before Nkrumah as a result of many factors including those relating to colonialism.

The courts remained free under the magistrates. The judges were appointed by the Judicial Service Commission. However, Nkrumah could dismiss any judge at any time for reasons that appeared to him sufficient.[16] Moreover, under the 1958 Preventive Detention Act (PDA), Nkrumah was empowered to detain Ghanaians for five years for actions he considered prejudicial to Ghana's security and its relations with other governments. In fact, Nkrumah dismissed judges very often and also many political opponents were detained.[17]

After discussing Nkrumah's notion of the role of the state machinery, it is now appropriate to present a general evaluation of his policy priorities.

All public expenditure was directly controlled by the central government. According to the available data (1958 to 1965), Nkrumah allocated 25.6 percent of the budget allocations to industrialization; 13.6 percent and 12.5 percent were allocated to education and health, respectively; and 9.1 percent to agriculture.[18] From this, it can be said that industrialization, education, health, and agriculture were his domestic policy priorities in that order.

Industrialization

Nkrumah pursued industrialization as a means of providing a better standard of living for the Ghanaians. There were also some political elements inherent in his industrialization programs. For example, Nkrumah maintained that an economically weak country would be a victim of neocolonialist tricks, and, more significantly, would be at the mercy of outsiders. Hence, in planning national development, the constant and fundamental guide, according to Nkrumah, is the need for economic independence. It is, therefore, not surprising that industrialization was his most pressing priority.

In addressing a CPP Study Group in Flagstaff House, Accra, Nkrumah provided several clues to his thinking and to an understanding of political and economic developments in Ghana by stating that:

> At this juncture, Ghana is not a socialist state. Not only do the people as yet not own all the means of production and distribution, but we have still to lay the actual foundations upon which socialism can be built, namely, the complete industrialization of our country. All talk of socialism, of economic and social reconstruction, is just empty words if we do not seriously address ourselves to the question of basic industrialization and agricultural revolution of our country, just as much as we must concentrate on our socialist education.[19]

This is scientific socialist thinking. The statement consistently exemplifies Nkrumah's pledge to the Marxist aim of state ownership of productive property. It also indicates that, like other modern Marxists, Nkrumah could not imagine a socialist state which is not also an industrial one. Industrialization, therefore, became a major theme.

Nkrumah stressed the point that energy is an indispensable element in industrialization.[20] What Nkrumah implied was that without energy, it would be difficult to lay solid foundations of industrial progress. Thus, industrialization presupposed electrification. Hence, Nkrumah's preoccupation with a grand project as the Volta River Project (VRP) and other schemes that would provide water power both for irrigation and electricity was not accidental.

In an effort to build Ghana into a modern industrialized state, Nkrumah launched the First and Second Five-Year Development Plans which covered the periods 1951 to 1956 and 1959 to 1964, and the Consolidated Plan bridged the two-year gap between the two plans, 1957 to 1959. For a successful building of a socialist state, Nkrumah believed that the human and natural resources would have to be developed through a series of development plans.[21] The plans could also eradicate completely the colonial structure of the economy. Once the human and natural potentialities were developed, the people would be able to break away, although gradually, from dependency. Building of such a self-sustaining economy would mean the need to have a balance in growth between industry and agriculture.[22] Such diversification could lessen Ghana's heavy dependence on cocoa.

There were three major aspects of Nkrumah's industrial strategy. First, industries were to be built which would make use of the local raw materials.

Secondly, these industries were designed to utilize cash crops and provide employment in rural areas. Thirdly, large industries were to be set up for the production of furniture.[23] And, for the industrialization program to work, Nkrumah proposed the building of the Volta Dam which would provide hydroelectric power for the industries and also to provide power to other neighboring African states. Considering the significance of the VRP, the largest industrialization scheme Nkrumah embarked on, a detailed analysis of the scheme will be pursued noting its political and economic implications in a separate chapter.

A major goal of Nkrumah in the pursuit of industrialization was to reduce the role of expatriate firms. Accordingly, he built such industries as two cocoa processing plants, two sugar refineries, a radio assembly plant, a meat processing plant, and a cement factory.[24] All of these industries were built to provide employment, to make use of local raw materials, and, consequently, to reduce the heavy reliance on foreign countries for these necessities.

Nkrumah, after independence, believed that for his political, economic, and social reconstruction to be successful, foreign economic activities had to be limited or controlled in Ghana and Africa generally. Nkrumah limited the activities of multinational corporations, whose presence Nkrumah believed undermined his socialist programs and the objectives of the CPP. Nkrumah accordingly dealt with giant monopolies like the Oppenheimer empire, the Anglo-American Corporation, De Beers, Unilever, and many others. Nkrumah did not allow them to operate in any exploitative way. For example, it was the state that set prices for commodities (control price). In fact, the multinational corporations were jubilant over Nkrumah's overthrow on February 24, 1966, because they disliked Nkrumah's strategy of phasing out the private sector through high taxes levied on the private sector.[25]

Since Nkrumah's socialism emphasized the public sector, it was not in the interest of the foreign investors to operate in Ghana. And through the imposition of high taxes on private industries, Nkrumah discouraged the private enterprise system, and this allowed the state to control all the strategic branches of the economy including public industries, raw materials, and heavy industries.

In the field of retail and wholesale trade, the Nkrumah regime established the Ghana National Trading Corporation (GNTC). This did not only curtail the role of expatriate firms in this sector but also alienated a large section of the Ghanaian petty bourgeoisie.[26] In the area of mining, the state took over complete control of the largest mining in Ghana, the Tarkwa Mines, in 1961. This takeover was effected to save jobs in the mines which had become unprofitable.[27] Here too, Nkrumah's socialist thinking is evident. His regime took over the mines not necessarily for profit, but to provide social service, employment.

As a result of the state's interference in the trade and mining sectors, the former colonial trading companies turned to the assembling of imported goods and the manufacture of light goods such as cutlasses. Unilever then started making soap inside Ghana, while Cadbury packaged tea and produced a malt chocolate milk. Also, Nkrumah tried to involve the state in the financial sector as well. He established the Ghana Commercial Bank and the Bank of Ghana, as well as independent Ghanaian insurance companies.[28] Prior to the establishment of these banks, foreign banks such as the Barclays Bank and Standard Bank were the major banks. Thus, the financial sector was no longer completely controlled by expatriates. With the establishment of the Bank of Ghana and the Ghana Commercial Bank, new types of investments were being financed. They made loans readily available to Ghanaian businessmen. Shipping was also partially put under state control, with the creation of the Black Star Line which as early as 1966 controlled 17 percent of Ghana's sea commerce.[29]

Furthermore, Nkrumah's industrialization policy emphasized the Ghanaian infrastructure. Contrary to the British objective of building communication systems to connect locations where they could benefit from economically, Nkrumah built the communication systems to connect towns and villages as a matter of public service, not for economic or profit motive. For example, there was a 59.8 percent increase in gravel roads between 1951 and 1961; 75.4 percent and 245.2 percent increases in post offices and telephones, respectively, between the ten-year period under consideration.[30] Understandably, the government controlled all communications in order to emphasize service to the Ghanaians rather than profit which is in accord with Nkrumah's pragmatic socialist principles. It is clear that Nkrumah intended state-owned enterprises to be the spearhead of Ghana's industrialization.

The backbone of the Ghanaian economy is cocoa. And, to be able to pursue the industrialization program depended, in a large measure, on the progress in the agricultural sector. Hence, Nkrumah saw a link between agriculture and industry.

Agricultural Policy

As indicated earlier, Nkrumah allocated only 9.1 percent of his budget to agriculture between 1958 and 1965. It is, therefore, accurate to say that Nkrumah's regime did not emphasize agriculture as strongly as industry, education, and health. But since the backbone of the economy was agriculture (Ghana earned from agriculture roughly 60 percent of the country's annual foreign exchange between 1956 and 1969, with even higher percentages in the early 1950s),[31] for a meaningful industrialization policy, Nkrumah should have stressed agriculture. In an agricultural country such as Ghana, the country depends on agriculture to provide revenues needed to finance industrialization and other social programs. Also, the agricultural sector provides market for the industries as the bulk of the population depends on agriculture. A majority of the population earn their incomes from agriculture with which they purchase the goods manufactured by the industries. Moreover, if the industries are to be efficient, they cannot rely on foreign raw materials but on local raw materials because they lack the capital to purchase foreign raw materials which are quite expensive. Also, the population will have to be fed and unless agriculture is well developed the country will have to import food. Thus, agriculture is significant in developing countries because it provides capital, market, and raw materials for the industries, and also it provides food for the entire population.

Like all other sectors, Nkrumah's agricultural policy was, mostly, based upon political rather than social considerations. Nkrumah employed various strategies to centralize and control the production and marketing of cocoa. An important institution which Nkrumah employed to centralize power in the marketing of cocoa was the Cocoa Marketing Board (CMB).

The Cocoa Marketing Board (CMB). The CMB was established by the British after the Second World War in response to the 1937/1938 cocoa boycott, an act of economic and political opposition by Ghanaian farmers against European cocoa buying firms which had collaborated to control prices paid to cocoa farmers. The CMB was established in 1947 to deprive the big firms of their functions of deciding producer prices and of the purchasing of cocoa independently. The big firms continued, however, to collect and supply credit, but now they were agents of the CMB.[32] Thus, in controlling the sale of cocoa to the world market, the state had become a direct extractor of the cocoa revenues.

As a result of the high prices of cocoa after the Second World War, the CMB enjoyed large surplus. So when Nkrumah came to power, it was only prudent for him to retain the CMB under state control. To make the point that the CMB under Nkrumah was entirely state controlled, it is necessary to describe briefly the cocoa marketing system.

At the center of the system stood the CMB which had the sole right to export and to buy for export. Two other institutions assisted the CMB in the exercise of its responsibilities. On the buying side, the United Ghana Farmers Council Cooperatives (often referred to as Farmers Council), which was state controlled, acted as the CMB's sole institution in purchasing cocoa beans from farmers and was responsible for its storage and transportation to the ports. Inspection and grading was undertaken by the Ministry of Agriculture's Produce Inspection Division which was independent both of the CMB and the Farmers Council. A system of buying centers was maintained. There were 1,400 of these centers in 1961. The farmer was paid a fixed price known as the producer price, formally fixed by the CMB which was subject to the prior approval of the Cabinet.[33] This was the price paid to the farmer at the buying station, wherever it may be, but the farmer himself had to bear any costs involved in moving his cocoa to the station. It must be said that some farmers, for financial reasons, had to carry their produce on the head for miles before getting to the produce station.

In placing the cocoa in the world market, the CMB employed the services of subsidiary organization, the Cocoa Marketing Company (Ghana Ltd.). The Cocoa Marketing Company formerly operated in London but in 1961, it was decided to set up a cocoa market in Accra, Ghana and its activities were then withdrawn from London.[34] Thus, all first-hand sales of Ghana's cocoa are still made in Ghana.

The CMB was, in effect, an instrument of governing policy. Although the composition of the CMB was nominally a representative one,[35] its policies were entirely under state control.

The farmers were unhappy about the low prices paid to them for their produce. Data is available as evidence that income was withheld from the Cocoa farmers. For example, during the 1957-1958 crop year, while the average price of exported cocoa was £G304 per ton, the CMB paid the farmers £G134 per ton, thus farmers were paid 44 percent of the world market's price. During 1958/1959 and 1959/1960, out of the £G280 and £G226 per ton the world market offered, the farmers received £G134 and £G112 per ton, respectively. Thus, during 1958/1959 and 1959/1960, the farmers received 48 percent and 49.5 percent, respectively of the world market's price. On the other hand, the financial record of the CMB for 1957 to 1960 was an enviable one to the farmers. For example, during this period, the CMB held large reserves, amounting in 1960 to £G26 million.[36]

The farmers were badly hit financially, especially in 1961 when cocoa prices fell alarmingly. The government refused to curtail its own expenditure and with the inevitable result that the cocoa farmers, the principal producers of the nation's wealth, were squeezed even more severely. In 1959, the Farmers Council (which was a state institution supposedly established to represent farmers), announced that the cocoa farmers had "agreed" to a reduction in their producer price of 12 shillings per load.[37]   But the truth is that the farmers never agreed to the reduction.

This new extraction brought the government an extra £G32.8 million.[38]   Also, the July budget of 1961 introduced compulsory savings in the form of development bonds which were, in theory, redeemable. The farmers were forced to provide a contribution levied at 10 percent of their producer price, while other workers in non-agricultural sectors contributed only 5 percent of their incomes. In October, 1963, the development bonds were abolished and replaced by income tax. Although most wage and salary workers in non-agricultural sectors got back their contributions, the Farmers Council announced that the farmers had "voluntarily" agreed to hand over their accumulated contributions to the government, an amount totaling over £G10 million. At the same time, the Council announced that the farmers had further "agreed" to another deduction from their producer price equal in amount to the abolished bond contributions.[39]

Also, in September, 1965, a further deduction was made, leaving the farmers with a price of 40 shillings per load for their cocoa.[40]   Thus, in ten years, the farmers' producer price had been halved. (In 1955, the producer price was 80 shillings per load.)[41]

Although significant in numbers and economic importance, the farmers were too far from the centers of political power to present any direct threat to the CPP regime. Undoubtedly, the agricultural measures damaged farmers' confidence. What we cannot forget is the fact that cocoa farmers also supplied a large proportion of the country's domestic food-stuffs. Intimidated by the party, and subjected to the arbitrary exactions of government, the farmers retreated into a defensive shell. CMB was used by Nkrumah as an important level of power for the control of cocoa farmers. The farmers, however, retaliated by reducing the production of foodstuffs, and this resulted in food shortages. For example, between March 1963 and September 1965, the prices of locally produced foodstuffs increased throughout the country by 82.3 percent. In the towns, the increase was even steeper. Over the same period, the prices of imported foods rose by 30 percent.[42] The worsening shortages drained away any remaining popular support for the regime and brought about a crisis of confidence within the party in the policies of the leadership.

The CMB's role was not restricted to the purchasing and marketing of cocoa produce, it also played a vital role in education. It was the primary government institution charged with the responsibility of awarding academic scholarships to students to pursue higher education. Its role in education is also indicative of the regime's interest in expanding its control.

The State Farms. To find a quick solution to the ever-growing shortages of food, Nkrumah decided to get the state involved in agricultural production. Thus, for the first time, Nkrumah embarked on socialized agriculture. In the past, the colonial government encouraged agricultural production and left it to the private sector.

Nkrumah established the State Farms Corporation (SFC) and the Workers' Brigade and charged them with the responsibility of introducing mechanized agriculture to increase agricultural productivity.[43] And, once, again, Nkrumah placed these corporations under state control.

The SFC was formally set up in January, 1963, although it had been effectively in operation during the previous year when it inherited the assets of the dissolved Division of Agriculture and the Agricultural Development Corporation. Twenty-seven farms had been set up during 1962 but by the following year, the Corporation was running over a hundred farms and employing 15,000 laborers, most of whom it had inherited from the dissolved agencies. Nkrumah assured the peasant farmers that their interests would not be subservient to those of the state farms. But it was clear that it was the latter he looked to, not only to produce plantation crops for export, but also to take over from the traditional farmers the task of providing the bulk of the country's foodstuffs.

It was the regime's contention that since these farms would be state controlled and managed by people trained in modern agricultural techniques, they were the easiest way of getting early results in agriculture.[44] And so out of the £G67.5 million total expenditure the Seven Year Plan envisaged for agriculture, £G10 million was allocated to the SFC, £G5 million to Workers' Brigade, and £G33 million to provide services for traditional farmers.[45] By 1965, out of the three million acres of total area of cultivated land in Ghana, the SFC had acquired control over 250,000 acres of it, although only 40,000 acres were actually cultivated. In addition, the Workers' Brigade held 280,000 acres of which less than one-tenth was actually farmed.[46] Thus, in a few years, the state agencies had acquired holdings amounting to about one-fifth of the entire cultivated area of the country.

From the above information, it is evident that Nkrumah emphasized the state agencies as a way of increasing agricultural productivity in Ghana. But, as it turned out, the state agencies failed. By 1965, only 0.5 percent of the country's food supply came from the SFC and Workers' Brigade Farms, despite the heavy investment in them.[47] And, as far as available statistics show, by practically every criterion, the performance of the SFC and the Workers' Brigade was inferior to that of traditional farmers.[48] The yield of produce in long tons per acre in 1965 was 0.21 compared with 1.17 on the peasant farms. In terms of output per worker, the state farms produced 0.59 tons per year compared with the traditional farmer's 2.18 tons.[49] Moreover, the state farms fell short of everyone of the modest production targets set for the crops they were engaged in cultivating. Throughout their existence (1963-1966), they never came close to breaking even, let alone making a profit.[50]

The state farms system suffered from both excessive centralization and inadequate control over its local operations. Its headquarters staff preferred life in the capital to service in the farms in the countryside. And, few of them knew what was going on down on the farms. The system of "district accounting stations" for local groups of farms made it almost impossible to make proper comparisons of costs and yields for individual farms, so no one knew whether money was being spent wisely or not. Individual farm managers sometimes sent to headquarters falsified or over-optimistic reports of their progress. Also, local farms were open to the interference of CPP officials who sometimes availed themselves of the produce for their own purposes.[51]

In spite of the various complaints against the inefficiency of the state farms and its officials, the government did not do much to revise the basic direction of its policies on the evidence abundantly supplied by experience. It was one thing to point out the state farms' shortcomings and quite another to correct them. The Corporation and the Workers' Brigade had become part of the official state establishment, secured against their failures and their critics by the will of the CPP and the president. Thus, overall, Nkrumah's agricultural policy received criticism from the farmers, the National Assembly, and the rest of the mass public.

Social Policy

To help develop Ghana, Nkrumah believed that the state should provide such essential social services as education and health.

Free Education. In pursuit of his socialist programs, Nkrumah engaged in the promotion of free education.[52] Education was made free from primary to college level. Free education was essential to any equality of opportunity for all young people, and equality of opportunity is in turn essential to the proper selection, training, and use of the most able professional and administrative personnel needed for both industry and government. Moreover, many parents and students were not good judges of the value of education to themselves and society. There were lots of parents who could not afford the costs of higher education, so Nkrumah made education free. Textbooks were supplied to students.

Between 1951 and 1961, there was a 211.9 percent increase in primary school enrollments, 141.7 percent increase in middle schools, 437.8 percent and 137.5 percent increases in secondary schools and training colleges, respectively. During the same period, the university students' enrollment increased by 478.8 percent. Table 2 shows the progress made in education.[53]

It is even reported that by 1966, Ghana had one of the highest enrollment rates in Africa. About 16 percent of the entire population were enrolled, whereas in Nigeria which had the second highest enrollment rates, only 5.7 percent of the population were enrolled. South Africa had 17.3 percent enrolled, but this can be misleading since this figure includes the affluent white population.[54] Education enabled Nkrumah to Ghanaianize the civil service.

Table 2
Educational Percentages in Ghana (1951-1961)

	1951	1961	Percentage of Increase
Primary schools	134,360	481,500	211.9
Middle schools	66,175	160,000	141.7
Secondary and technical schools	3,559	19,143	437.8
Teacher training colleges	1,916	4,552	137.5
University students	208	1,204	478.8

Source: *Kwame Nkrumah* (London: Panaf, 1974), p. 95.

Free Health Services. As part of Nkrumah's pragmatic socialism, he provided health services free of charge. A certain minimum amount of medicine, hospital care, medical attention, dental treatment, and so forth were treated as a free good in the socialist economy Nkrumah was trying to build. This clearly signifies the ideological aspect of Nkrumah's socialism.

There was a 159 percent increase in the number of hospital beds between 1951 and 1961. Rural and urban clinics increased from one in 1951 to 30 in 1961. There was also a 220.5 percent increase in the number of doctors and dentists between 1951 and 1961.[55] Free medical care was very significant because most workers could not afford the fees, and even those who could afford were hesitant to go to the hospital in order to save money. The free health services to children meant the creation of the complete equality of opportunity Nkrumah envisioned in a socialist system. A child who receives insufficient medical care is often handicapped for life. Community health has an economic value to every individual. If Nkrumah had not made health services free, it would have meant the spread of more communicable diseases caused by victims who may either refuse or could afford to pay for the costs of curing them. It can, therefore, be asserted that free health could materially increase the productivity of labor by improving the health of the average worker. (See the evaluation section of this chapter for data on doctors per population and also on infant mortality.) After discussing Nkrumah's domestic policies, we will now turn to his foreign policy.

Foreign Policy

Nkrumah's foreign policy took two major directions. First, he devoted a great part of his foreign policy to liberation struggles in all parts of Africa. Moreover, as a Pan-Africanist, he hoped to see continental independence followed by the creation of a continent-wide United States of Africa. This way, he thought, could forestall the balkanization of the continent foisted on her peoples by the colonialists whose interest it was to continue economic exploitation and political domination in a new form of colonialism. Secondly, Nkrumah tried to create a world audience for the African cause. Thus, not only did he pursue the "African personality" phenomenon (this helped create the African presence through visible Africans, not foreigners), but also took active part in the decolonization process through the UN. Moreover, as an ardent supporter of decolonization, he also proclaimed to be non-aligned. We will now discuss:

1. His policy in Africa, and
2. His policy outside Africa.

Policy in Africa

Nkrumah took concrete approaches towards Pan-African unity. One line of approach was aimed at generating support for Pan-African unity. This took the form of All-African Peoples Conferences (AAPC) which included the December, 1958 AAPC held in Accra.[56] A significant feature of these meetings was that they were popular or people's movements and were nongovernmental with the representatives coming from trade unions, political parties, and other African membership organizations. The resolutions adopted during the 1958 AAPC held in Accra included the proposal to establish a permanent secretariat in Accra, Ghana to accelerate the liberation of Africa from imperialism and colonialism, and also to work towards the emergence of a "United States of Africa."[57] The resolutions adopted were largely unacceptable to governments because the resolutions represented positions too far to the left. Thus, it can be said that the influence of the AAPC for uniting the peoples of Africa into a nation was, at best, marginal.[58]

Another line of approach to Nkrumah's dedication for Pan-African unity involved agreements among governments. Still working towards Pan-

African unity, on November 23, 1958, Nkrumah and Sékou Touré, president of the newly independent Republic of Guinea, announced the formation of a Ghana-Guinea Union. The main objective of the Union of Independent African States which they created was: "to build a free and prosperous African community in the interest of its peoples and world peace."[59] Membership, as defined on May 1, 1959, was to be open to all independent African States or Federations which were prepared to adhere to the principles on which the Union was based. Resident ministers were to be exchanged, and economic relationships explored. The economic relationship was stimulated by the promise of a grant of £10 million by Ghana to its poorer partner, Guinea.

At the end of 1960, the Union was joined by President Modibo Keita of Mali after Mali's break with Senegal. On July 1, 1961, the three republics (Ghana, Guinea, and Mali) issued 14 articles of a "Union of African States" as the "nucleus of the United States of Africa."[60] Nkrumah was elected president of the Union, thus putting Ghana in the forefront of Pan-Africanism. The Union faded away as a result of a number of practical problems including those relating to geography and language. For example, Touré spoke French and no English, and Nkrumah spoke only English. Even though the Ghana-Guinea-Mali faded away, it has left a legacy. (As a Ghanaian in the United States, I am treated very well by people from Guinea and Mali and likewise Ghanaians treat Guineans and Malians as brothers.)

The emergence of conflicting regional groupings after 1960 tended to undermine the All-African unity. In January, 1961, the Casablanca Group was formed. Its members included Ghana, Guinea, Mali, UAR, Morocco, and later Algeria became a member. With the exception of Morocco, the Casablanca Group took similar ideological positions on some important issues. For example, they were closer to the East than the West, although they officially claimed to be non-aligned; they supported Lumumba in the Congo crisis; they condemned Israel and also demanded Algerian independence.[61]

A second regional grouping was the Brazzaville Group, officially called the Union of African and Malagasy States (AMU), were composed of the former French colonies with the exception of Togo, Mali, and Guinea. The AMU joined with eight other states–Nigeria, Sierra Leone, Tunisia, Ethiopia, Congo (Leopoldville), Tanganyika, Somalia, and Togo to form the

Monrovia-Lagos Conference.[62] Like the Casablanca bloc, the Monrovia-Lagos Conference was non-aligned but took a more friendly position toward the West. The Monrovia-Lagos Conference was primarily concerned with economic and social development through economic cooperation. Thus, while the Casablanca bloc favored Pan-African unity based on political integration of sovereign African states, the Monrovia-Lagos Group opposed political integration and emphasized solidarity and good neighbor relations.

Nkrumah was one of the key personalities behind the May, 1963 Addis Ababa Conference which brought all the 32 independent African states together. It was at this conference that the Organization of African Unity (OAU) was formed.[63] Unlike the 1958 AAPC (which was non-governmental), the 1963 Addis Ababa Conference was governmental.

Despite Nkrumah's preference for a political union, the independent African states present at the 1963 Addis Ababa Conference drew up a modest charter which stressed the sovereignty of the individual members and reached an agreement on the principle of non-interference in the internal affairs of the states. In fact, when the Conference took the practical step of establishing a Liberation Committee of representatives of nine African states to assist nationalist groups in colonial jurisdictions and South Africa, Ghana was excluded. Thus, the first of the Pan-Africanist was ignored. (This could have been Ghana's West African location.)

There were other activities Nkrumah engaged in which aided the building of his continental outlook. Apart from the exchange of ambassadors with other African countries, Nkrumah encouraged exchange of visits between Ghana and other African states. For example, women's and youth organizations, where they existed in states which had exchanged diplomatic representatives with Ghana, were invited to send representatives to tour Ghana. Indeed, in 1965 a team of Congolese women exchanged visits with a similar team from Ghana.[64]

Furthermore, Nkrumah used sports to highlight the Pan-African cause. Nkrumah placed great emphasis on inter-African sports. Inter-African games and soccer competition were organized and Nkrumah provided an African Soccer Challenge Cup.[65]

From the above discussions, it can be concluded that unlike other African leaders, Nkrumah agitated for a political union of all African states rather than just economic cooperation. Nkrumah's emphasis on the need for a United States of Africa made him very unpopular among African statesmen as they interpreted such a move as encroachment on their sovereignties.

Policy Outside Africa

It cannot be denied that during Nkrumah's regime, Ghana's Pan-African posture put her in the forefront of African affairs. It helped to raise the black man in the eyes of the world, and Africa took on a new image and prominence, which is usually described by Nkrumah in terms of the African personality.[66]

In the practice of Ghana's external relations, Nkrumah identified a number of policy areas which included:

1. Decolonization through the UN
2. The role of the Commonwealth
3. Non-alignment, and
4. Establishing the African presence on the international scene (for example, his abortive Hanoi trip).

The UN. Admission to the 13th Session of the United Nations General Assembly as a sovereign independent state in September, 1957 gave Ghana an opportunity to work with like-minded states for the decolonization of the African continent. Ghana was free to link up with the independent states noted for their anti-colonial policies, such as the United States, Canada, India, and the Eastern European countries. This necessitated the policy of non-alignment.

The Ghana UN mission had special responsibility to maintain close links with the African UN Group established as a result of the first conference of the Independent African States.[67] By this means, Ghana sought to harmonize its anti-colonial policies with those of other African states.

Also on important questions in the UN concerning African states, Ghana played a visible role.[68]   One of Ghana's advantages was its membership in the UN Security Council, which began in January 1962.[69] Ghana was, therefore, in a position to initiate the Rhodesian independence issue in the Security Council even though other African states wanted the Rhodesian question raised in the General Assembly, where they could contribute.[70] Even though Ghana wielded no real influence on the Council, there is no doubt that it brought considerable attention to Ghana and Africa generally. By 1964, Ghana's prestige and recognition at the UN had reached such a level that her representative, Alex Quaison-Sackey, was elected president of the General Assembly for the 1964-1965 term.[71]

The Commonwealth. As a former British colony, Ghana joined the Commonwealth. Since membership of the Commonwealth was not by force but at will, Nkrumah did not have any reservations joining it.

The Commonwealth, Nkrumah believed, posed no threat to the sovereignty of Ghana; it was rather a forum to maintain peace, tranquility, and understanding between nations. Nkrumah also believed that the Commonwealth could help bring an end to colonialism and also help the newly independent countries to become economically viable.[72] As an ardent supporter of decolonization, he continued to see himself as non-aligned even after becoming a member of the organization. (His specific activities in the Commonwealth are presented in the next section.)

Non-alignment. In dealing with countries outside Africa, Nkrumah embarked upon a policy of "positive neutralism" as he put it. What Nkrumah meant was that he did not want Ghana or any other African country to get involved in the cold war between the East and the West.[73]

Supporting anti-colonialism and at the same time maintaining good relations with the Western powers was a difficult game for Nkrumah. This was obvious in the area of non-alignment. By historical tradition, Ghana's political future was bound up with that of Britain with which she shared the Commonwealth fellowship. Nkrumah showed great interest in Commonwealth meetings which he attended himself. His most significant contribution to the Commonwealth connection was his proposal at the 1964 conference for the establishment of a Commonwealth Secretariat.[74] Despite his great interest in the Commonwealth, he broke off relations with Britain to support the 1965 OAU resolution over Rhodesia's unilateral declaration of independence.[75] Here too, his Pan-African commitment was clear.

Ghana's ethnic ties with neighboring French-speaking states made close relations with France practically indispensable. All the same, Nkrumah condemned the Sahara atom test by the French.[76] This made the development of relations with France and French-speaking states difficult. The French tested again at the end of 1960. Nkrumah then announced that Ghana had frozen all French assets in Ghana. Actually, the French businessmen were really not affected; they had found ways to circumvent the measures. Exactly two weeks later, the French assets were unfrozen. Indeed, Nigeria, assuming Ghana would break relations with France, expelled the French ambassador. But Ghana did not.[77] It became clear that Nkrumah had failed a very important test: to restrict foreign business interests. This action by Nkrumah also shows that he was pragmatic and knowing that Ghana could not provide the capital herself, he did not want to discourage foreign investment.

Insofar as the United States was concerned, her strong support at the United Nations for the process of decolonization in Africa and her position as the greatest economic force in the post-war world made the forging of close links between her and Ghana an imperative necessity. (But Nkrumah did not do this.)

Nkrumah's decision to draw closer to Eastern Europe was a means of expressing in concrete terms Ghana's freedom of action. Ghana found herself standing between the two world giants, compelled by her need to draw on both for technical and economic aid. Thus as a non-aligned state, Ghana could maximize her aid as she could obtain loans from both the East and the West.

In August and September 1961, Nkrumah toured Europe and attended the Belgrade Conference of non-aligned powers in order to emphasize his commitment.[78] No official visit was made to the East German Democratic Republic, as the West German representative in Ghana had made it clear that this would be regarded by his government as a hostile act. As Nkrumah was hoping at the time to obtain £2,000,000 loan from West Germany for a second bridge over the Volta, in order to provide a direct fast route to Togo, Nkrumah agreed to their wishes. This understanding did not, however, prevent Nkrumah from making a brief stop-over in East Berlin while on a visit to Prague.[79] This clearly indicates that Nkrumah was a pragmatic politician. And as an ardent Pan-Africanist, he was sometimes prepared to compromise in the name of Pan-African unity.

African Presence. Nkrumah referred to "African presence" and "African personality" as concepts predicated on the principle that Africans should be heard through Africans. And, Nkrumah's external policies were largely aimed at enhancing the African personality. A major projection of his African personality is manifested in his abortive Hanoi trip.

The war in Vietnam had been discussed at the Commonwealth Prime Ministers' Conference in June, 1965. At the meeting, the prime ministers had expressed their intention of sending a mission of their own, comprising the heads of government of the United Kingdom, Ghana, Nigeria, and Trinidad and Tobago to explore the peace-making possibilities, but this proposal came to nothing. In early June, a British junior minister, Harold Davies, paid a five-day visit to Hanoi. In December, the Pope made special appeals for the restoration of peace.[80]

In spite of the failure of the Commonwealth peace mission and the Pope's appeals, President Nkrumah believed that the prospect of peace was not altogether bleak. It would certainly be a great credit to the "African presence," and the developing world in general, if the initiative for peace in Vietnam could come from that source.

Nkrumah's concern for Vietnam was greatly stimulated by a personal invitation to visit Hanoi, which he received in July, 1965 from President Ho Chi Minh. Nkrumah's associates and friends made efforts to dissuade him from making the journey, all of which proved unavailing.[81] Nkrumah seemed to feel that if he failed to honor Ho Chi Minh's invitation, he would let down an Asian leader for whom he had the greatest respect. He also indicated that if he did not go to Vietnam, he would seem to be lacking in courage and resolution. But it was also clear that Nkrumah believed if he was successful, this could enhance his own prestige and influence in the world and also enhance his motive of gaining more international recognition for Africa. And, as it turned out, the consequence of the unfinished journey is now history; he was overthrown while he was on route to Hanoi.

Evaluation of Nkrumah's Regime Performance

For a fair assessment of Nkrumah's regime performance, I will suggest five central criteria.

First, the growth of the economy must be considered as all third-world countries consider growth to be indispensable. For a long time, per capita Gross National Product (GNP) was used as an important measure of economic efficacy because GNP could provide quantitative indicators. But in recent years, GNP has come under numerous criticism. For instance, the GNP offers no information on actual levels of well-being and also says nothing about income distribution. Furthermore, the rising levels of mineral production, especially oil (and in the case of Ghana gold) depend very little on the performance of the regime.

I believe that to measure growth in African states, a close examination of the growth record in peasant agricultural sectors is more appropriate. (The term "peasant" is used loosely because of how it is used in the literature. In the Ghanaian case, not all farmers were peasants, there were some who belonged to the middle class. In Ghana, the language does not make the distinction. Peasants and middle class people who were farmers were simply referred to as "farmers.") This is because a majority of the population live in the rural sector; and also rising rural productivity will increase the incomes of the poorest sector of the population. Thus, to measure growth in Ghana, we will look at the growth record in cocoa production during Nkrumah's time and then compare to that of his successors. Between 1959 and 1966 (Nkrumah's era), there was an average annual growth rate of 4.76 percent in cocoa production[82] compared to -2.36 percent growth from 1969 to 1976 (his successor's time).[83] It can, therefore, be said that based on growth in cocoa production, Nkrumah did better than his successors.

Second, equality of distribution deserves discussion. This criterion will be measured in terms of state-fixed wages for skilled and unskilled labor, state provided amenities such as schools and medical facilities, and also state-fixed prices for major commercial crops such as cocoa.

Table 3 on the following page illustrates the levels of earning for skilled and unskilled workers between 1964 and 1974.[84] The average earnings of unskilled workers, on the whole, increased more slowly than those of skilled workers throughout the period, with the most noticeable inequalities revealing after 1966. Between 1964 and 1966 (that is, during Nkrumah's time), both skilled and unskilled workers had comparable incomes and therefore similarly felt the pinch of inflation. But after 1966 when inflation got worse, skilled workers did not feel the strain the same way as the unskilled ones, because the former's nominal income was increased while the latter's remained about the same. Based on this data, one can posit that income was more equitably distributed during Nkrumah's regime than during his successors.

In the area of education, we will simply inspect the enrollment rates in Ghana during the time of Nkrumah and compare these figures to other neighboring African states. It is reported that by 1966 Ghana had one of the highest enrollment rates in Africa with 16 percent of its total population enrolled. The second highest was recorded in Nigeria where only 5.7

Table 3
Consumer Price Index (CPI) and Indices of Average Nominal
And Real Earnings of Skilled and Unskilled Workers
In Ghana (1964-1974) (1963=100)

Year	CPI	Skilled Workers		Unskilled Workers	
		Nominal Earnings	Real Earnings	Nominal Earnings	Real Earnings
1964	119.7	100.0	83.5	100.0	83.5
1965	151.3	100.0	66.1	100.0	66.1
1966	171.4	102.3	57.7	100.0	58.3
1967	157.0	109.7	69.9	107.7	68.6
1968	169.7	117.9	69.5	115.4	68.0
1969	181.8	127.0	69.9	115.4	63.5
1970	188.8	134.0	71.0	115.4	61.1
1971	206.0	140.1	68.0	115.4	56.0
1972	226.5	173.7	76.7	153.8	67.9
1973	274.7	--	--	198.4	72.2
1974	315.3	--	--	307.7	97.6

Source: F. Lisk, "Inflation in Ghana, 1964-1975: Its Effects on Employment, Incomes and Industrial Relations," *International Labour Review,* 113, No. 3 (May-June 1976), p. 369.

percent were enrolled. South Africa had 17.3 percent enrolled but this figure includes the affluent white population.[85]

Health services will be measured by looking at doctors per persons and also infant mortality. By 1960, there were 21,000 persons per doctor[86] compared to 14,110 persons per doctor in 1966[87]; and by 1973, there were 9,842 persons per doctor.[88] It can be concluded from this that Nkrumah increased substantially the number of medical doctors between 1960 and 1966.

Infant mortality is calculated as the number of live births per 1,000 within the first year of births. Between 1957 and 1960, infant mortality was 97.45 per 1,000[89] compared to 156 per 1,000 between 1970 and 1975.[90] Thus, infant mortality was lower during Nkrumah's time than his successors.

The state-fixed price for cocoa paid to farmers in 1955/1956 was 80 shillings per load. By 1962/1963, the farmers were paid 54 shillings for the same quantity.[91] Thus, in less than ten years, Nkrumah almost halved the farmers' producer price.

Moreover, Nkrumah's 1961 compulsory savings measure discriminated against the farmers. While farmers were forced to provide a contribution of 10 percent of their producer price, workers in non-agricultural sectors had to contribute only 5 percent of their incomes.[92] Even though between 1959 and 1966, cocoa production growth rate increased by 4.76 percent, between 1962 and 1966, there was a growth of -1.79.[93] Clearly, these discriminatory measures damaged farmers' incentive and confidence.

Third, participation may need to be included. This criterion will be determined by considering the level of citizen access and involvement in the decision-making process through such mechanism like party. The degree of political participation was low in Ghana at the time of Nkrumah as there was only one political party, the CPP. The opposition was silenced. The CPP turned its members and the other organizations into weapons for control rather than instruments of participation.

Fourth, autonomy and self-reliance must be considered. In reality, this goal of self-reliance can only be met partially as autarchy is impossible to attain. To measure the extent of Ghana's self-reliance we will look at its foreign debt burden and also the extent of Ghana's control over its natural resources.

Between 1962 and 1966, Ghana witnessed an average debt burden of ¢305 million (cedis) per year[94] compared to ¢588.68 million between 1969 and 1973.[95] Thus, there was excessive foreign debt during the time of Nkrumah's successors.

Nkrumah had complete control of the largest mining in Ghana, the Tarkwa mines.[96]

The dependency theorists will argue that the interest on external capital is the inevitable fate of the weak, peripheral state. Even though Nkrumah reinforced and deepened the peripherization through the more active welcome to foreign investment, he repeatedly and continuously maintained a radical anti-imperial international posture. Thus, he was completely conscious of the inescapable dependency condition and even detailed that in his concept "neocolonialism."[97]

Finally, the preservation of human dignity needs consideration. This criterion will be determined by the absence of large-scale, state-directed repression of individuals. Here, we will look at the evidence of political repression such as detention and imprisonment of individuals. Another evidence is the emergence of refugees.

Direct evidence of political repression is readily available in the U.S. State Department, which compiles annual reports on the status of human rights around the world. This document has reported that among the human rights abuses in later Nkrumah years were the extensive use of Preventive Detention Act, and also the imprisonment of several hundred political prisoners.[98]

Emigration (as used here) does not refer to those who leave their countries for economic reasons (brain drain) but those who flee because their lives are in jeopardy. Data are difficult to obtain for Ghana's political refugees because there are only a small number of Ghanaian political refugees. This does not, in any way, imply that Nkrumah's rule was free of human rights abuses, but that the number of Ghanaian political refugees did not reach anywhere near those of other African countries such as Ethiopia and Zaire.

In conclusion, the competency of the Ghanaian bureaucracy, Africanization of cadres and rapid expansion of industry, higher education, and health services are few instances of Nkrumah's efforts to build Ghana into a competent socialist state which would be capable to carry out all development plans. The Civil Service was very competent, but whether or not it was efficient is another matter. Up to this day, Ghana is credited as one of the few African countries with the most competent intellectuals.

Nkrumah's role in history is an ambiguous one. By the cold measurement of economic growth statistics and human rights record, his regime was a miserable failure; and the disillusionment suggested that at the human level also he signally failed to achieve his goals. And, yet he cannot be dismissed as a failure quite so readily. Despite the disillusionment, Ghanaians have shown a sense of national identity stronger than most African countries. Also, Ghanaians have been occupying all high governmental positions, that some other African states have as yet even contemplated. If Nkrumah bears much of the responsibility for Ghana's economic and social problems today, he cannot be denied some credit for the successes that Ghana has enjoyed.

There were improvements in growth. Yet the standards of living, industrialization, and modernization were of modest proportions. Agriculture showed little improvement. Nkrumah's Ghana was neither the best nor the worst in Africa at that time. We do not think of Nkrumah as the maker of economic miracles.

Nkrumah received higher marks in equality of distribution. He got rid of the English ruling class. Ethnicity was no basis for upward mobility. Schools and health facilities were improved for all.

Participation was higher in the 1950s when Nkrumah was fighting for independence than in the 1960s when he resorted to authoritarian rule.

Autonomy and self-reliance is difficult to achieve for a poor country. Nkrumah did well to free Ghana from the worst aspects of neocolonialism.

Nkrumah enhanced human dignity by his conscious effort to enhance the place of Africans in the world. His fight for decolonization and also Quaison-Sackey's role as the president of the U.N. General Assembly undoubtedly intensified the African presence in world affairs. Nevertheless, Nkrumah deprived Ghanaians of human rights during the end of his regime. His PDA of 1958 well illustrated this.

Based on the five criteria: growth, equality of distribution, participation, autonomy and self-reliance, and preservation of human dignity, it can be concluded that, under the circumstances, Nkrumah's regime performed well.

As evidence of his contribution to Ghana's development, we will now turn to his Volta River Project.

Endnotes

[1] *Programme of the Convention People's Party for Work and Happiness* (Accra, Ghana, 1962).

[2] Ben Amonoo, *Ghana 1957-1966: The Politics of Institutional Dualism* (London: George Allen & Unwin, 1981), pp. 41-65.

[3] Ibid.

[4] Ibid., p. 51.

[5] Ibid., pp. 50-65.

[6] Ibid., pp. 66-73

[7] Ibid., pp. 100-102.

[8] Max Weber, *The Theory of Social and Economic Organization* (New York: the Free Press, 147), p. 363.

[9] Ibid., pp. 224-225; and Anthony M. Berret, "Laws and Leaders in the New States," *Africa Today* (1966), pp. 12-14.

[10] See *Parliamentary Debates,* XVI, No. 35, col. 1682 (1959).

[11] Dennis Austin, *Politics in Ghana 1946-1960* (London: Oxford University Press, 1970), p. 259.

[12] Weber, *The Theory of Social and Economic organization,* p. 361.

[13] Ibid.

[14] Ibid.

[15] Kwame Nkrumah, *Revolutionary Path* (London: Panaf, 1973), p. 182

[16] Austin, *Politics in Ghana 1946-1960,* p. 413.

[17] Robert E. Dowse, *Modernization in Ghana and the USSR: A Comparative Study* (New York: Humanities Press, 1969), pp. 91-93.

[18] Andrzej Krassowski, *Development and the Debt Trap: Economic Planning and External Borrowing in Ghana* (London: Overseas Development Institute, 1974), p. 159.

[19] Kwame Nkrumah, *Address to CPP Study Group in Flagstaff House* (Accra, 1961).

[20] Kwame Nkrumah, "Some Aspects of Socialism in Africa," *Pan Africa* (Nairobi), April 19, 1963, pp. 13-14.

[21] *Kwame Nkrumah* (London: Panaf, 1974), pp. 191-192.

[22] *Speech to Launch the Seven Year Development Plan,* 11 March 1964; and Nkrumah, *Revolutionary Path,* p. 186.

[23] *Kwame Nkrumah,* p. 102.

[24] Ibid., p. 93.

[25] Ibid., pp. 107-108.

[26] Barbara Callaway and Emily Card, "Political Constraints on Economic Development in Ghana," in Michael F. Lofchie (ed.), *The State of the Nations: Constraints on Development in Independent Africa* (Berkeley: University of California Press, 1971), p. 86.

[27] *Ghana: Five Year Development Plan* (Accra, January 1977), Part II, p. 231.

[28] Callaway and Card, "Political Constraints on Economic Development in Ghana," p. 80.

[29] Ibid., pp. 80-86.

[30] *Kwame Nkrumah,* p. 95.

[31] Peter C. Garlick, *African Traders and Economic Development in Ghana* (London: Clarendon Press, 1971), p. 145.

[32] Rhoda Howard, *Colonialism and Underdevelopment in Ghana* (New York: Africana Publishing Company, 1978), pp. 206-227.

[33] *Ghana Cocoa Marketing Board at Work,* 4th edition (Accra, 1963), pp. 6-12.

[34] G. B. Kay, *The Political Economy of Colonialism* (London: Cambridge University Press, 1972), pp. 244-246, 252-272.

[35] In August 1963 the Board consisted of a Chairman, the General Manager, and the General Secretary of the Farmers Council, the Production Manager, and representatives of the ministries of finance and trade. All these are government appointees.

[36] Walter Birmingham, I. Neustadt, and E. N. Omaboe, *A Study of Contemporary Ghana: The Economy of Ghana,* Vol. I (Evanston: Northwestern University Press, 1966), p. 369.

[37] Trevor Jones, *Ghana's First Republic 1960-1966* (London: Methuen & Company, 1976), p. 243.

[38] Ibid.

[39] A. W. Osei, one of the few surviving opposition members, described the manner by which the Council secured the farmers' "agreement"; "Whenever there is a conference, the Farmers Council calls only the officials to meet, and the Council asks the officials to convey the decision they take at the meeting to the farmers. At the meeting the head of the Council just gets up and says 'we are going to do this and that.' " (*Off. Jnl. Parl. Debs.,* 28 October 1963, col. 353.).

[40] Garlick, *African Traders and Economic Development in Ghana,* p. 20.

[41] Ibid.

[42] *Quarterly Digest Statistics* (Ghana, Ministry of Information: Central Bureau of Statistics, Vol. XVI, Table 55, 1969).

[43] Jones, *Ghana's First Republic 1960-1966,* p. 150-151.

[44] *Ghana: Seven Year Development Plan: Report (1963-64 to 1969-70),* p. 75.

[45] Jones, *Ghana's First Republic 1960-1966,* p. 248.

[46] Ibid., p. 249.

[47] Ibid., p. 250.

[48] The State Farms Corporation failed to produce reliable statistics of its own operations. The University of Ghana assessed independently the performance of the Corporation in *Background to Agricultural Policy* (Proceedings of a seminar organized by faculty of Agriculture, University of Ghana, April 1969).

[49] *Ghana: Seven Year Development Plan: Report for the Second Plan Year 1965*, p. 19.

[50] "On a nationwide basis they were still, at the time of the 1966 coup, unable to meet their operating costs, much less contribute any return on the initial capital invested." (Marvin P. Miracle and Ann Seidman, *State Farms in Ghana*, Land Tenure Center, University of Wisconsin, L.T.C. No. 43, March 1968.)

[51] During a debate in August 1965, the Chairman of the Corporation admitted that this kind of interference was widespread. He told of how "a district commissioner went to a farm and suggested that he should be supplied with one hundred tubers of yam a week. People in high positions sometimes came to our farms and instead of buying a few pounds of rice, they buy bags of it. I know that many of these men have large families but you will agree with me, sir, that in Ghana no family, however large, can consume one hundred tubers in a week." (*Off. Jnl. Parl. Debs.*, 27 August 1965, col. 107.)

[52] *Kwame Nkrumah*, p. 95.

[53] Ibid.

[54] Ibid., p. 96.

[55] Ibid., p. 95.

[56] Austin, *Politics of Ghana, 1946-1960*, p. 396.

[57] Ibid.

[58] J. Leo Cefkin, *The Background of Current World Problems* (New York: David McKay Company, Inc., 1967), p. 294.

[59] George W. Shepherd, *The Politics of African Nationalism: Challenged to American Policy* (New York: Praeger Inc., 1962), p. 96.

[60] Austin, *Politics in Ghana, 1946-1960*, pp. 395-397.

[61] Thomas Hovet, Jr., *Africa in the United Nations* (Evanston: Northwestern University Press, 1963), pp. 52-60.

[62] Scott Thompson, *Ghana's Foreign Policy: 1957-1966* (Princeton: Princeton

University Press, 1963), pp. 209-214.

[63] Thomas A. Howell and Jeffrey P. Rajasooria, *Ghana and Nkrumah* (New York: Facts on File Inc., 1972), p. 95.

[64] Michael Dei-Anang, *The Administration of Ghana's foreign Relations, 1957-1965* (London: The Althlone Press, 1975), pp. 39-40.

[65] Ibid., p. 40.

[66] Ibid., pp. 49-50.

[67] Thompson, *Ghana's Foreign Policy: 1957-1966*, p. 41.

[68] Dei-Anang, *The Administration of Ghana's Foreign Relations, 1957-1965*, p. 50.

[69] Thompson, *Ghana's Foreign Policy: 1957-1966*, p. 197.

[70] Ibid., p. 391.

[71] Dei-Anang, *The Administration of Ghana's Foreign Policy Relations, 1957-1965*, p. 12.

[72] Kwame Nkrumah, *I Speak of Freedom* (New York: Praeger Inc., 1961), pp. 100-101, 144.

[73] Ibid., p. 143.

[74] *Interviews: CF-103, 10 November 1965, London; CF-106.* This was one of Nkrumah's most imaginative diplomatic exercises, and one which much impressed the British, however reluctant they were to develop the secretariat.

[75] *Interviews: CF-106, CF-14, 10 November 1965,* London.

[76] Thompson, *Ghana's Foreign Policy: 1957-1966*, p. 98.

[77] *P.R. #295/60, 5 April 1960, #311/60, 7 April 1960.*

[78] "Conference of Heads of State and Government, Belgrade," *Ghana* (Accra, 1961), p. 99.

[79] Thompson, *Ghana's Foreign Policy: 1957-1966*, pp. 402-403.

[80] Ibid., pp. 409-411.

[81] Howell and Rajasooria, *Ghana and Nkrumah*, p. 113.

[82] *U.N. Statistics,* Vol. 14, 1962, p. 106; *U.N. Statistics,* Vol. 17, 1965, p. 119.

[83] *U.N. Statistics,* Vol. 29, 1977, p. 107. The decline had started during the latter period of Nkrumah's regime as a result of the compulsory savings program.

[84] F. Lisk, "Inflation in Ghana, 1964-75: Its Effect on Employment, Incomes and Industrial Relations," *International Labour Review,* 113, No. 3 (May-June 1976), p. 369. Also see Kodwo Ewusi, *the Distribution of Money Incomes in Ghana,* University of Ghana Institute of Statistical, Social and Economic Research, Technical Publication Series, No. 14 (Accra, 1971), pp. 11 and Table 2, p. 15.

[85] *Kwame Nkrumah* (London: Panaf, 1974), p. 96.

[86] *World Development Report,* 1979, p. 168.

[87] *U.N. Statistics,* Vol. 20, 1968, p. 701.

[88] *U.N. Statistics,* Vol. 26, 1974, p. 781.

[89] *U.N. Statistics,* Vol. 16, 1964, p. 52.

[90] *U.N. Statistics,* Vol. 28, 1976, p. 79.

[91] Garlick, *African Traders and Economic Development in Ghana,* p. 20.

[92] *Off. Jnl. Parl. Debs.,* 28 October 1963, col. 353.

[93] *U.N. Statistics,* Vol. 14, 1962, p. 106; *U.N. Statistics,* Vol. 17, 1965, p. 119; *U.N. Statistics,* Vol. 121, 1969, p. 98.

[94] *U.N. Statistics,* Vol. 20, 1968, p. 622.

[95] *U.N. Statistics,* Vol. 26, 1974, p. 687.

[96] *Ghana: Five Year Development Plan* (Accra, January 1977), Part II, p. 231.

[97] Immanuel Wallerstein has carefully detailed the inevitable framework of the contemporary "international capitalist system," in his article, "Dependence in an Interdependent World: the Limited Possibilities of Transformation within the Capitalist World Economy," *African Studies Review,* 17, No. 1 (April 1974), pp. 1-26.

[98] House of Representatives, Committee on Foreign Affairs and Senate, Committee on Foreign Relations, *Country Reports on Human Rights Practices for 1979,* submitted by Department of State, 4 February 1980; House of Representatives, Committee on International Relations, *Country Reports on Human Rights Practices,* submitted by Department of State, 3 February 1978. Also, refer to various country reports compiled by Amnesty International from 1960-1984. See especially *Amnesty International Report: 1979* and also *Amnesty International Report: 1982* (London: Amnesty International Publications, 1979 and 1982, respectively).

Discussion Questions

1. Some scholars have argued that Nkrumah's Pan-Africanist creed came back to haunt him. Is this a convincing statement? Why?

2. Briefly describe the conflicting approaches and the emergence of the conflicting regional groupings in the late 1950s that led to the formation of the Organization of African Unity in 1963.

3. What criteria would you use to assess Nkrumah's regime performance, and why?

Chapter 5

The Volta River Project (VRP)

A s stated in the previous chapter, the industrialization of Ghana was Nkrumah's most important priority. He, therefore, spent a substantial portion of public expenditures on promoting his industrialization program. For the industrialization program to work, Nkrumah proposed the building of the Volta River Project (VRP) which was to provide hydroelectric power for the industries, agriculture (irrigation), and also to provide power for neighboring African states. The chapter is primarily devoted to a detailed analysis of the VRP, the largest industrialization scheme undertaken by Nkrumah. The chapter is divided into five major sections:

A. The background of the VRP. This will include the discussion of the history of the project, its financing, and description of the dam and its distribution of hydroelectric power.
B. An analysis of the motives of the major actors. They were: the United Kingdom, the Nkrumah's government, the United States government, the Kaiser Corporation, the World Bank, and finally the Ghanaian people.
C. Discussion of the political, social, and economic costs and benefits that came out of the scheme.
D. Report of an interview with Dr. Gilbert White (chairperson of the UN mission sent to Ghana to study the feasibility of the VRP in 1968).
E. The conclusion of the study of the VRP.

The Background of the VRP

History of the VRP
The history of the Volta scheme falls into four phases:
   a)   The first phase started in 1915 with the discovery of bauxite on the Kwahu plateau. This encouraged a South African engineer, Duncan Rose,

to start some scientific investigations into the possibilities of harnessing the waters of the Volta River for the generation of electricity to produce aluminum.[1]

b)   The second phase saw the work of the Preparatory Commission from 1953 to 1956. The Preparatory Committee was set up by the British to survey the development and operation of the local bauxite mine, to analyze the problems of communication, and to construct the dam.[2] The Preparatory Commission Report stated that: "The VRP will accelerate the trend from rural towards industrial communities.[3] Thus, the emphasis was on industrial development as opposed to rural development, to the extent of creating a modern community.

c)   The third stage saw the visit of the then Prime Minister of Ghana, Dr. Kwame Nkrumah, to President Eisenhower of the U.S. in 1958 requesting help.[4] President Eisenhower agreed, in principle, to give the assistance upon a further feasibility study conducted by an American consultant, Kaiser Engineers. They submitted their report in 1959 suggesting: 1) the changing of the main dam from Ajena to Akosombo, 2) the building of the smelter at Tema instead of Kpong, and 3) that the alumina should be initially imported instead of processing it from local bauxite. They were requested to form an alumina company that would consume sufficient power to justify the project. This gave birth to the formation of the Volta Aluminum Company Limited (VALCO). The contract for the construction of the dam as given to a consortium of Italian corporations, Impregilo.[5]

d)   The fourth phase focused on the construction of the dam and formation of a statutory body in 1961 to be known as the Volta River Authority (VRA). The VRA was responsible for the construction of the dam. Its chairperson was the president of Ghana, Nkrumah. Its functions included:

1.   The development of the fishing potentialities of the lake and a route for commercial transportation.
2.   The resettlement of the people displaced.
3.   The administration of the township of Akosombo as a local government agency.
4.   The research in conjunction with other agencies, into the development prospects and problems of the lake, including hydrobiological studies, public health, and shore line agriculture.[6]

Financing of the VRP

The construction of the dam was estimated at £70 million of which Ghana was to provide 50 percent with the rest coming from foreign loans. Table 4 illustrates how the finances of the VRP were arranged.[7] Because the arrangement was multilateral, it was definitely to Nkrumah's advantage for it is difficult for any single country to control the recipient country.

Table 4
Sources of Finances for the Volta Dam

Source	Term	Interest Rate	Amount £ Million
International Bank for Reconstruction and Development	25 yrs.	5¾%	16.8
Agency for International Development (USA)	30 yrs.	3½%	9.6
Export-Import Bank (USA)	25 yrs.	5¾%	3.6
Export Credits Guarantee Department (UK)	25 yrs.	6%	5.0
Ghana Government	(Equity Investment)		35.0
		Total	70.0

Source: *Kwame Nkrumah* (London: Panaf, 1974), p. 103.

The Dam and the Distribution of Hydroelectric Power

The hydroelectric system consists of a rock-filled dam, a power house, and a transmission network. The dam is situated at Akosombo, about 100 kilometers from the mouth of the river and in a narrow gorge separating the Kwahu plateau from the Togo ranges. (See following map.)

The dam is about 150,000 square miles with two-thirds of it in Ghana, with one-third of the waters coming from no fewer than five West African countries–Upper Volta (now Bourkina Faso), Togo, Dahomey, Ivory Coast, and Mali. The reservoir is 280 feet above sea level and 440 feet high from its foundation.[8] It has created a lake of about 480 kilometers long and with a total storage capacity of 168 million cubit meters. And it is said to be the largest man-made lake in the world.[9] The power house contains six turbines which drive six generators for the production of power. The dam was opened in 1965 and until 1972, only four of the turbines and generators

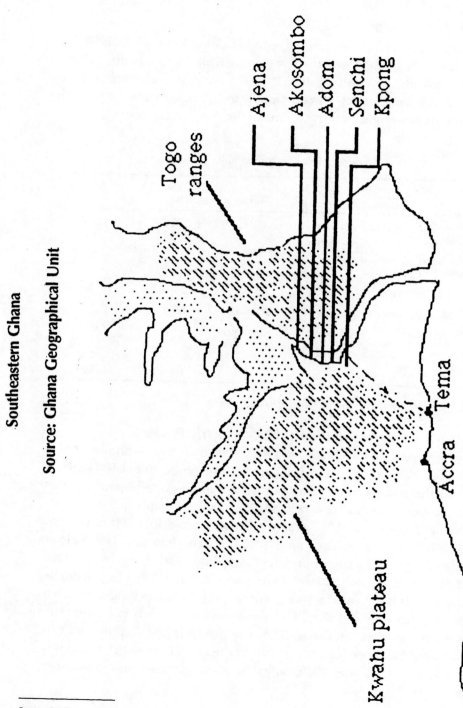

Southeastern Ghana

Source: Ghana Geographical Unit

had been installed for a capacity of 512 MW. But in December, 1972, the last two were installed, raising the total capacity to 768 MW.[10] Looking at the gigantic nature of the dam, it can be said that Nkrumah really wanted Ghana to break away from dependency.

A natural distribution network of 800 km of 160 kv line carries the power to substations located at Kpong, Volta, Valco smelter, New Tema, Achimota, Cape Coast, Prestea, Takoradi, Tarkwa, Obuasi, Kumasi, Konongo, Nkawkaw, Tafo, Akwatia, and Winneba, where the voltage is stepped down after transmission to the required voltage.[11]

The VALCO remains the largest consumer of the Akosombo power and consumed about 69.6 percent of the total output in 1973. Other users are the Electricity Corporation of Ghana and the mining companies.[12] To date, that is, in 1995, not many homes benefit from the power, but it is hoped that under the Rural Development Project, extensions will be made to cover most parts of the country, to bring it home to the suburban centers and villages, as well as to the rural industries. The problem is inadequate capital necessary for the extension work.

As a Pan-Africanist, Nkrumah had the motive of distributing the power to other African states. Nkrumah's VRP is exporting power to the Republics of Togo and Benin. For this reason, a transmission line of 294.4 km has been built from Akosombo to Lome and then to Cotonou. This extended power transmission was switched on in 1972 and formally dedicated in 1973. Power is sold to these countries through the Agence Communauté Electrique du Bénin. Ghana sold about 99,723,000 KW-hours energy or about 3 percent of its total energy of about 3,871,500,000 KW-hours generated in 1973 to the two countries. With the extensions being made in the supply of power in Ghana, the exports of power and the increased consumption of the major consumers (VALCO increased consumption by 16.0 percent in 1973 over 1972 consumption, Electricity Corporation also increased consumption by 9.8 percent), it was estimated then that by 1980 the capacity of the Volta Dam will be fully committed.[13] The magnitude of this project is indicative of Nkrumah's big development plans for Ghana and Africa. Because of political instability, this project proved futile in terms of providing him with substantial political support. Nkrumah was overthrown on February 24, 1966, a month prior to the inauguration of the VRP.

The Main Actors of the VRP

The various actors involved in the VRP had motives that differed substantially. The major actors were: the United Kingdom, the Nkrumah's government, the U.S. government, Kaiser Corporation, the World Bank, and the Ghanaian people.

The United Kingdom

The reason for U.K.'s interest in the VRP becomes clear on reading the British White Paper Cmd 8702 of November 1952. Even the title of this document–The Volta River Aluminum Scheme–gives a strong indication of the British motives. The paper starts with an account of U.K.'s requirements of aluminum and forecasts that these requirements would increase at about 5 percent a year. The scarcity of aluminum on the world market at the time made the British government take an interest in the scheme and so appointed a group of consulting engineers, Sir William Halcrow and Partners, to investigate the viability of the project. They recommended that the gorge at Ajena should be sited for the dam and that an aluminum smelter should be built at Kpong and a port at Tema. The British accepted the report towards the end of 1952 and appointed a Preparatory Commission to make a further thorough investigation.[14]

Moreover, the White Paper Cmd 8702 of November, 1952 contains an important statement:

> *"The chief difficulty is the heavy demand of electric power which the extraction process makes. Unless cheap power is already available in large quantities, any major new development of aluminum producing capacity involves at the same time the large scale development of power–normally as things are, hydroelectric power. This means in practice that large-scale expansion of aluminum production under present processes can only take place in connection with major power developments.[15]*

Thus, the reason for U.K.'s interest in the VRP was Ghana's bauxite. But the British had to develop power for its production. The White Paper failed to clarify whether Ghana would actually benefit from the scheme as proposed.

The Nkrumah Government's Attitude

The VRP was a high priority in Nkrumah's government. Nkrumah stated that the VRP was "designed to produce the electrical power for our great social, agricultural and industrialization programme."[16] The importance Nkrumah attached to the role of electric power in a developing country may be argued from the following quotes from Ghana's Legislative Reports:

> *I have always been convinced that an abundance of cheap electric power is the soundest base for the expansion of industry in a country such as ours.... My government is determined to develop the hydroelectric potential of Ghana to its maximum.[17]*

Thus, the rationale behind the VRP was that it would provide abundant supplies of electricity. Electricity was seen as a necessary requisite for industrialization. The Nkrumah government did not see the aluminum side of the venture as the primary aspect of the project. It was the other uses to which the electricity could be put that attracted them. But in order to get the project going, Ghana needed foreign capital and foreign expertise which it did not have. It may seem paradoxical that Nkrumah, the author of "Neocolonialism," should have been so keen on welcoming foreign capital and foreign expertise into Ghana. Nkrumah did not have alternatives. There was no African Development Bank for him to turn to as it was not established until September 10, 1964. So he had to turn to countries outside Africa. Less developed countries need development but lack the capital. The capital, therefore, has to come from the outside.

The United States Government

Why did the U.S. government involve itself in the VRP? R. G. A. Jackson stated that the political factors were paramount. Ghana represented the first of the newly independent African states (Ghana became independent on March 6, 1957), and the U.S. was anxious to gain influence in Africa. Here was an ideal opportunity. The desire to achieve greater standing in Africa was heightened by memories of events in the United Arab Republic where the Suez crisis had led to the withdrawal of the American and British funds from the Aswan High Dam. As a result, Russian economic support had been used for that project.[18]

In a statement before the House Committee on Foreign Affairs,

G. Mennen Williams (U.S. Assistant Secretary of State for African Affairs in the 1960s) explained, in response to a question of why the U.S. gave so much assistance to Nkrumah's government, in view of Nkrumah's expressions of hostility, said:

> It is our estimate that in the long run there are favorable factors that ... will prevail. This is an area where the British developed a very soundly based civil service, a well-trained military.... The middle class is a sizeable one, and the amount of free enterprise is considerable. Their most important crop is cocoa. These are all middle class, independent farmers. I think when you put the thing in balance that over the long run we could hope for a government which would be at least non-aligned.[19]

Ghana enjoyed great prestige as the first Sub-Saharan African country to gain independence. Also, Washington believed that Ghana was not yet lost to Soviet influence and the U.S. wanted to strengthen its influence in Africa.

The Kaiser Corporation

Kaiser's concern was not a broad one of fulfilling human needs but a narrow one of producing cheap aluminum. By involving itself in the VRP, the Kaiser Corporation was able to gain access to cheap hydroelectricity, and was able to place itself in a strategic position to obtain some of Ghana's supply of bauxite.[20] That Kaiser was not particularly interested in Ghana's desire for development is indicated by the way in which it rejected the Bui Scheme as an alternative to the VRP. The Bui Scheme was a hydroelectric project. The proposed Bui Scheme, a smaller one than Akosombo, had been assessed at the request of the Ghana government in the Halcrow Report of 1951 and in the Preparatory Commission Report, but to no avail. The Bui Scheme was not large enough to interest non-Ghanaians, it was rather the VRP that attracted them.

Kaiser too did not raise any enthusiasm for the Bui Scheme, and clearly stated the reason:

> This development (Bui), due to small river flow and the remote location, would be relatively economical only for the public supply of electricity. The very large block of low cost power for electrochemical production is not available here.[21]

The emphasis here is on Kaiser's interest in aluminum production rather than Ghana's desire for electricity.

The World Bank

The World Bank sent a mission in early 1957 to review the economic conditions in Ghana. The mission questioned the advisability of undertaking the VRP at that time. Subsequent World Bank reports remained lukewarm on the issue of whether to go ahead with the scheme or not.[22] Also, the World Bank insisted that the agreed upon electricity price be fixed for 30 instead of the 50 years proposed by VALCO. In the subsequent master agreement between the Ghana government and VALCO, a clause was included that the World Banks's approval was needed for any future alteration in the price of electricity.[23] The World Bank was saying that Ghana was locking itself into a price which can be harmful over such a long time. Moreover, the price was too inflexible, and also it is difficult to have projection for 50 years of what a fair price will be.

Thus, the World Bank seems to have been acting as a buffer between the Ghana government and the competitive commercial interests involved in the VRP. Here too, the vulnerability of Nkrumah is clear.

The Ghanaian People

The main participants of the project have been dealt with. What about the others, those affected by the scheme? The VRP did not arise out of Ghanaian initiative so most Ghanaians did not have any aims as such to fulfill through the implementation of the project. Instead, they had received from others or acquired for themselves a set of expectations about what the project would mean to Ghana, generally. Some expected the project to be beneficial, while some thought otherwise. A Ghanaian economics professor, J.C. De Graft Johnson, stated that the scheme was

> fraught with many socioeconomic problems such as the displacement of people from the land, the diversion of labour from agriculture, and other fields of economic activity, including the mining of other minerals, the possible increase in river blindness, and further disintegration of existing social units.[24]

What of the Ghanaians who were to be directly affected by the VRP, those people living in the area to be flooded by the new lake? They thought that their land was being stolen by the government to be used in a different way.[25] This taking of the land is in congruence with Nkrumah's notion of the role of central government to control land just as it was in the African traditional communal ownership system in which land was managed for the common good.

It must be said that the implementation of the whole project, thought of as far back as 1915, has not been as smooth as perhaps the foregoing details may indicate, for there have been many obstacles both at the planning, negotiation, and construction stages. The project was unduly delayed under the colonial government. Planning and a series of feasibility studies alone took 42 years (from 1915 to 1957) compared to the period of eight years (from 1957 to 1965) when under African administration expediting the implementation enabled the government to complete it.

Furthermore, a series of undermining activities by political opponents made negotiations for financial assistance from the rich nations difficult. And, in addition to the lack of capital, skilled labor, and the required technology, Nkrumah was forced to accept terms under which the project was carried out, which would be unacceptable today, but were quite acceptable in 1957. For instance, the formation of VALCO with no Ghanaian participation, and the subsequent profit repatriation, coupled with the employment of foreign labor and slow development of local skills are all indicative of Nkrumah's vulnerability.

The problem of building transmission lines through the tropical rain forest with the dense trees and climatic hazards were also some of the serious problems faced.

Costs and Benefits of the VRP

Having covered the main aspects of the VRP, it is important to appreciate what was involved in building a giant project like the Akosombo hydroelectric scheme in a small developing country like Ghana, which has limited resources that were competed for by numerous industries that were springing up.

Costs
By costs, I refer to all other alternative gains which Ghana had to forego in order to build the scheme. For this purpose, I will recount:

    a) The huge sum of £70 million that was raised for the project could have given Ghanaians more hospitals, schools, or better roads, all of which would have made life easier and happier at that time, but £70 million was not available for these purposes.

b) Also the labor, tools, machines, and other factors of production that were engaged in this project could have produced more cocoa for more foreign exchange which could have been used to improve the economy.

c) Resettlement: Akosombo Dam created a huge lake covering about 8,500 km², the largest man-made lake in the world. The area covered by the lake was inhabited by 80,000 people living in 739 villages and comprising of more than 1 percent of Ghana's population. The people displaced were mostly subsistence farmers who grew mostly cocoa (they lost about 2,400 hectares under the lake). River fishermen were also displaced.[26]

The Preparatory Commission Report recommended that the people to be moved should be compensated in cash so that they could resettle. It argued that this would have the advantage of retaining communal initiative and encouraging people to help themselves, instead of looking to government for assistance in all matters.[27] Thus, if people were to be resettled, the report suggested that no matter what plans might be made in the initial stages, constant pressure would be directed towards increasing the scope of the operations, with consequent increased spending.

However, this recommendation was rejected, because of India's experience in the Damodar Valley Project, in which 91 percent of the people to be resettled chose cash compensation in preference to accepting land for land and house for house. The result was mass influx to Indian cities and later efforts to recolonize the people from the streets of the cities to the farmlands had little success.[28]

Further reasons for the rejection of a self-help scheme were the large numbers of people involved and the lack of time to mobilize them. It was found to be easier to bring in building workers to erect resettlement houses. So instead of imposing some kind of self-help scheme upon the victims of the lake, they were encouraged to participate in the government's resettlement program. Those who did not want to participate were given cash to resettle.[29] These were the people who became known as the "Gone Elsewhere" villagers (the G.E.s).

The type of house built for the resettled people was called a "core" or "nuclear" house. It consisted of a concrete floor, lancrete block walls, and a corrugated aluminum roof. (Lancrete is concrete made with soil as the major constituent.) It was called a "core" house because although sufficient floor space was provided for two rooms and two porches, only one room was to be constructed before the settlers moved in. The rest of the house was to be completed by the settlers themselves. It is reported that by the end of 1970, 11,985 "core" houses had been built. Also, some 800 households that had chosen to be resettled did not obtain a "core" house.[30] No record is available on what happened to them, but presumably they went elsewhere. Many houses remained uncompleted, because they were difficult to complete. Nkrumah had not anticipated these problems. And, of course, we should expect these shortcomings to play a significant part in the annihilation of his personality cult Ghanaians so respected.

Large numbers of settlers found themselves in untenable positions in the resettlement villages. The houses were too small for the large families in Ghana. There was the inevitable problem of overcrowding. The average number of people per room in 1968 was 2.2 compared with 1.4 before the villages were flooded.[31] Also, complaints of physical discomforts were rampant. It got very cold at night in the resettlement houses, but no heat or blankets were provided by the government.[32]

It was not only dissatisfaction with the housing that led to the large numbers of settlers moving out of their new villages, but also serious problems connected with the viability of farming around the settlements.

The issue of compensation was equally a sad one. The average amount paid per individual family was $819. Some of them were paid as little as $3 for their old houses. Moreover, most of the compensation payments were heavily delayed.[33]

d) Health: There have been serious health hazards associated with the VRP. Three diseases of major incidence were river blindness, sleeping sickness, and malaria. Even though Nkrumah made efforts to reduce the incidence, he had no significant success.[34] Because of these problems, one may say without any fear of contradiction that the human factors were not duly considered when the VRP was planned. One should expect Nkrumah, a supporter of socialism, to have paid more attention to the welfare of the victims of the VRP, but this was not the case.

On the economic side, some Ghanaians argued that the VRP is one of the major causes of inflation in Ghana today. The project itself is not directly productive, but rather it is to provide the base for industrial development. But, consequently, the huge amount injected into the project increased the multiplier effects on the economy of the initial purchasing power without increasing output by the same margin both in the short run and long run, at least up to today. Hence, it has been argued that the VRP is inflationary.

Benefits

There were some benefits that came out of the VRP for which Nkrumah has to be given credit.

Power. Despite the aforementioned foreseeable sacrifices, the choice fell on this project because of the singularly important role power plays in the development of a nation. Large-scale production of today is dependent not on availability of power, but on availability of *cheap* power. It is power that turns the machines in the factories, hospitals, mines, and so forth. Hydroelectricity is a cheap source of power. The most important benefit, therefore, to be derived from the VRP is the availability and use of cheap power in Ghana's industrialization program. To this end, Nkrumah, to say the least, had good intentions to lead Ghana towards development.

Employment. The fact that the VRP guaranteed people employment is an undoubted success of Nkrumah's socialism. The VRP gave employment to over 6,000 Ghanaians initially,[35] but the result of such an initial employment on total volume of employment could be seen in multiples, according to the multiplier principle. By raising the general purchasing power, output would be increased. This is, however, based on the assumption that producers would normally respond to the increase in demand. But the producers' response to increased demand has always been low in Ghana for obvious reasons, such as lack of adequate infrastructure, capital, raw materials, spare parts, and so forth. Thus, inflation was the response.

Fisheries. In contrast to the resettlement scheme, the development of a fishing industry on the Volta Lake has been a success. This has become possible as a result of essentially individual initiative. It was only in 1971 that the Ghana government began a scheme to provide facilities for the fishermen. It can be commented unequivocally that private enterprise which Nkrumah spoke against through his socialist principles was working, at least, momentarily. But this did not alter Nkrumah's ideology.

At first, the expectations of the VRP for fishing were very low; a figure of 18,000 ton catch per year was quoted.[36] In fact, production from the lake reached a peak of 60,000 tons in 1969 before settling down to a level of

38,000 tons in subsequent years when the lake had become ecologically stable. This annual catch of 38,000 tons may be compared with an estimated figure of 10,000 tons for the annual catch from the Volta before the VRP was built.[37] Fish caught from the lake sell for an average price of 33 cents per kilogram and the average value of a year's catch is $11.1 million. We may infer then, that this is a significant benefit since the value of fish caught compares with a figure of $32.8 million total value obtained from Akosombo-produced electricity in 1969.[38] The Volta River's production of fish is also significant when compared with Ghana's other sources. The total marine catch was estimated as 119,000 tons in 1969. And Ghana imported 18,700 tons of fish valued at $6.8 million in the same year. Thus, in 1969, Ghana's total fish consumption was 137,700 tons. The catch from Volta Lake therefore satisfies approximately 43.6 percent of Ghana's demand for fish.[39]

Agriculture. Irrigation with the waters of the lake helped farmers on the Accra and Afram plains to overcome the most difficult natural obstacle in agriculture–aridity.[40] With certain crops like maize, tomatoes, onions, and so forth, more than two harvests a year became possible, thus engaging the farmers throughout the year, removing the seasonal unemployment characteristic of places with alternating dry and wet seasons. Varied crops could now be grown to feed the people, local industries, and also for export. For instance, the vast sugar cane estates around Asutuare promote the local manufacture of sugar and provide molasses for the traditional distilling of alcohol. To this extent, Nkrumah's industrialization was working. The major limiting factor is the prevalence of water-borne diseases, but if the research going on is successful, they can be controlled to allow the people to get nearer the lake where intensive irrigation can be practiced.

Also, during the rainy season, the lake expands and when it retreats during the dry season (November to July), it exposes the peripheral areas it covered during the rainy season. Such areas are called "drawdown" areas and are useful for agriculture because the lake deposits silt there during the floods.

Lake Transportation. As a transportation route, the lake linked the North with the South; opened up the area and removed the inaccessibility which had been the most serious obstacle in the economic development of that area between the Kwahu plateau and Togo ranges in the southeastern part of Ghana. Already, a pilot scheme for traffic of both passengers and cargo has been started under a commercial transport company–Volta Lake

Transport Company, with 51 percent government shares. This was incorporated in Ghana in 1970 and formally inaugurated in October, 1971.

Wildlife and Tourism. Volta Lake is an imposing body of water and its scenic attractions are enhanced by the winding nature of its many arms. The impressive engineering achievements of the dam and power house are already drawing a stream of visitors. Clearly, a Ghanaian wildlife reserve would enhance its tourist value if it would be sited on the lake shore where the normal tourist interest of wildlife reserve would be complemented by the lake's attraction.[41]

Overall Cost-Benefit Analysis. According to the World Bank Report, the projected revenues and costs from 1965 to 2014 would be $345.9 million and $332.6 million respectively, using a discount rate of 5 percent.[42] Thus, the benefit to cost ratio is equal to 1.04. It can, therefore, be said that apart from the human and social costs, in purely economic terms, the VRP is a viable one.

In reality, the VRP energizes the economy even though the dam itself had only marginal benefits, such as providing hydroelectric power for industry and agriculture.

Dr. Gilbert White's Perceptions of the VRP[43]

In 1966, the military regime which came to power saw that the VRP was not being utilized to its fullest potential. As a result, it requested the UN to help Ghana realize the full usefulness of the VRP. In response to this request, the UN sent three academicians with Dr. Gilbert White as the chairperson.[44]

In response to my question of how he felt about the VRP, Professor White, in a lengthy discussion, emphasized that to him the VRP was a "savage" undertaking. By "savage," he meant that the planners of the VRP failed to account for the needs, capabilities, and the health of the Ghanaians. He admitted that the VRP had indeed improved agriculture, utilized cheap labor, and also increased fisheries, but at the expense of human health. Thus, it was a cutthroat project. Hence, "savage."

The problem Dr. White saw was how to minimize damages and improve fisheries at the same time. To him, this objective is very difficult to realize, and therefore, concluded that Ghana should not have undertaken such a large project in the first place. He further added that when Ghana decided to undertake the venture, it failed thoroughly to investigate the human aspects. Rather, it concentrated more on the engineering, economic, and most importantly, on the political aspects. It is very likely that Nkrumah's Pan-African urge made him pursue the project, especially when he recognized that some of the hydroelectric power could be transported to other African states.

Dr. White further said that the Ghana government under Nkrumah failed to help the settlers become adapted to the new physical, social, and economic environment. He stressed the point that human settlement is a particularly complex process which demands time, effort, and resources. He also said that Nkrumah adopted the scheme in haste. Dr. White thinks that there should have been systematic background investigations of the rural society to be affected by the creation of the lake, along with the objective appraisal of the extent of human resources development required by the technical and economic change foreseen. All these, Nkrumah failed to do. He went on to say that also required were supporting facilities, social controls, and the development of strong leadership. All these ingredients were missing.

One of the reasons why Ghana was at the brink of total bankruptcy towards the end of Nkrumah's reign was the large sums of money it spent on the VRP. Unquestionably, this contributed to his overthrow by the military in 1966.

Finally, when I questioned Dr. White about the prospects of the VRP in the future, he responded that the VRP has a future but it will take time. And, that, before it reaches its full potential, Ghana will continue to pay the price. And even after the VRP has reached its full usefulness, Ghana will continue to trade off between economic development, political concerns, and human concerns.

Conclusion

It was probably an unwise decision for Nkrumah to undertake such a big venture, but since Ghana has already pumped lots of resources into the VRP and the dam has been built, it should not be abandoned. To improve upon the VRP, the Ghana government should reconsider and pay considerable attention to the human aspects. It should also pump resources into research and build hospitals or clinics too help cure and prevent the diseases caused by the creation of the VRP. To obtain funds for this, it should press for a better price for the electricity sold to VALCO. Also, the terms of the master agreement should be renegotiated or altered so that VALCO would also be subjected to the normal company tax. The money received from these altered financial arrangements could be spent on alleviating the disruption caused by the resettlement scheme. Whether the money will be spent in this way will depend on the internal political situation in Ghana. These moves would, of course, be resisted by VALCO but they have to be carried out to help lighten the burden of the VRP.

Ironically, Nkrumah was overthrown by the military a month before the inauguration of the Volta Dam. The VRP was suspended, thereby halting Ghana's progress towards industrialization. The VRP was aimed at creating new acres of new agricultural land and also to provide kilowatts of hydroelectric energy needed for Nkrumah's industrialization pursuit. I am confident that when Ghana becomes fully industrialized in the future, then opponents will also recognize the significant role the VRP played and Nkrumah's name will always be associated with it. To these ends, Nkrumah's VRP was successful as over time the benefits will be obvious.

Endnotes

[1] James Moxon, *Volta: Man's Greatest Lake* (New York: Praeger Publishers, 1969), p. 49.

[2] Ibid., p. 76.

[3] *Preparatory Commission Report, the Volta River Project*, Vol. 1, 29, (1956), pp. 16-20.

[4] *President Eisenhower and Prime Minister Nkrumah: Joint Statement,* White House, Washington (July 1958).

[5] Moxon, *Volta: Man's Greatest Lake,* p. 101.

[6] *Volta River Development, Act* 1966, Government of Ghana.

[7] *Kwame Nkrumah* (London: Panaf, 1974), p. 103.

[8] Moxon, *Volta: Man's Greatest Lake,* p. 23.

[9] Ibid., pp. 84-92.

[10] Ibid.

[11] R.H. Lowe-McConnel, *Man-made Lakes* (London: Institute of Biology Symposium No. 15, n.d.), p. 102.

[12] Moxon, *Volta: Man's Greatest Lake,* pp. 202-214.

[13] Ibid.

[14] British White Paper Cmd 8702, *The Volta River Aluminum Scheme* (November, 1952).

[15] Ibid.

[16] Kwame Nkrumah, *Dark Days in Ghana* (London: Panaf, 1968), p. 77.

[17] *Ghana, Legislative Assembly Reports,* March 1959.

[18] R.G.A. Jackson, *The Volta River Project: Progress* (Unilever), No. 4 (1964), pp. 146-161.

[19] C. Allen and R. W. Johnson, eds., *African Perspectives: Papers in the History, Politics and Economics of Africa* (London: Cambridge University Press, 1970).

[20] Moxon, *Volta: Man's Greatest Lake,* p. 93.

[21] Henry J. Kaiser and Company, *Reassessment Report on the Volta River Project for the Government of Ghana* (Oakland, Calif. 1959).

[22] IBRD, *Preliminary Appraisal of the Volta River Hydroelectric Project* (Washington: World Bank, 1957).

[23] IBRD, *Appraisal of the Volta River Hydroelectric Project* (Washington: World Bank, 1960, 1961).

[24] J.C. De Graft Johnson, *Background to the Volta River Project* (Kumasi: Abura Printing Press, 1955), p. 30.

[25] Lowe-McConnel, *Man-made Lakes,* p. 102

[26] Rowena M. Lawson, "An Interim Economic Appraisal of the Volta Re-settlement Scheme," *Nigerian Journal of Social and Economic Studies,* 10(1) (March 1968), pp. 95-109.

[27] Preparatory Commission, *The Volta River Project,* Vol. 1, 1956.

[28] Keith Jopp, *The Story of Ghana's Volta River Project* (Accra, 1965).

29   Robert Chambers, *The Volta Resettlement Experience* (London: Pall Mall Press, 1970), p. 48.

30   *Volta River Authority (VRA), Annual Report,* 1970.

31   FAO/UNDP, *Volta Lake Research, Ghana: Interim Report* (Rome, 1971).

32   Chambers, *The Volta Resettlement Experience,* p. 74.

33   E.K. Afriyie, Report on the Preliminary Social Survey of Foue Krachi Area "G.E." Villages, *Volta Lake Research Project,* May 1969.

34   B.B. Waddy, "Health Problems on Man-made Lakes," *Geographical Magazine* (April 1966).

35   John Bird, *Report on Volta River Scheme* (Accra: West African Aluminum Limited, 1949).

36   Preparatory Commission Report, *The Volta River Project,* Vol. 1, 1956.

37   F.M.K. Denyoh, "Fisheries of the Volta Lake," in W.C. Ackermann, G.F. White, and E.B. Worthington, *Man-made Lakes: Their Problems and Environmental Effects* (Knowville, Tenn.: International Symposium on Man-made Lakes, 1971), n.p.

38   *Volta River Authority (VRA), Annual Report,* 1976.

39   Lowe-McConnel, *Man-made Lakes,* p. 29.

40   Chambers, *The Volta Resettlement Experience,* pp. 185-189.

41   *Volta River Project. Report on the Mid-term Project Review Mission,* DP/SF/301/GHA, 10 December 1969.

42   *World Bank. Cost-Benefit Analysis: Volta River Project,* 1976.

43   Gilbert White, University of Colorado, Boulder, Colorado. Interview, 22 March 1984.

44   Dr. Gilbert White is an Emeritus Professor of Geography and Director of the Institute of Behavioral Science, University of Colorado, Boulder. He is the president of the International Council of Scientific Unions' Scientific Committee on Problems of the Environment (SCOPE). In 1968, he was the chairperson of the UN mission sent to Ghana to study the feasibility of the Volta River Project.

Discussion Questions

1. Discuss the domestic and international politics which surrounded the building of the Volta River Project.

2. Was the Volta River Project a viable project or a savage one, and why?

Chapter 6

The Problems Leading to Nkrumah's Decline

This chapter will concentrate on the problems which eventually resulted in a coup d'état which ousted Nkrumah's regime on February 24, 1966. The leaders of the coup were: Major-General Kotoka, commander of 2nd Infantry in Kumasi; Colonel Afrifa, staff officer of the 2nd Infantry in Kumasi; and Inspector-General J.W.K. Harlley, head of the Ghana Police Service. The major causes for the coup according to its perpetrators were related to Nkrumah's internal policies and external policies. Internally, they accused Nkrumah for having led Ghana toward a one-man regime, his inability to abolish social inequalities, Nkrumah's waste of resources, corruption, economic deterioration of Ghana, and also Nkrumah's lack of respect for the traditional institutions (chieftaincy). Nkrumah's external relations with communist countries and his reliance on foreign aid, and his Pan-Africanism came under attack.

In addition to the military and the police, there were other forces opposed to Nkrumah's approach to Ghanaian modernization. They were the chiefs, the former opposition parties like the NLM and UP, as well as most of the mass public. All these forces felt antagonized by the CPP government and therefore supported the military. The chiefs had virtually lost all their functions. The opposition made conscious moves to support the military because differences between Nkrumah and the opposition remained. The peasant farmers and other workers suffered greatly as a result of Nkrumah's economic policies. Even though the operation to remove Nkrumah was undertaken by an oligarchic group in the military and police service, the operation received support because the leaders of the coup cited problems with which the mass public could identify. We will now discuss these problems.

Internal Problems

Among the reasons the leaders of the coup cited were:

Nkrumah's Violation of Civil Rights and Liberties

The military faction that overthrew Nkrumah accused him of leading Ghana toward a one-man regime. To sustain his charisma, Nkrumah resorted to arbitrary decision-making.[1] Colonel Afrifa wrote that through legal and parliamentary manipulations, supported by the largely illiterate mass of the CPP, Nkrumah managed to consolidate virtually all power in his own hands. This effectively undermined the UP, the NLM, and other opposition parties. Afrifa cited the Preventive Detention Act (PDA) of 1958 as one of Nkrumah's major instruments for silencing the opposition elements.[2] The PDA empowered Nkrumah to make the decision to detain members of the opposition parties or CPP members who opposed his programs for five years without trial if he deemed it to be in the interest of national security.[3]

Another instrument of control, according to Afrifa, was the 1960 constitution which the CPP railroaded through parliament without adequate debate and had the effect of endowing Nkrumah with virtually absolute power and of laying the foundation for making him president for life. This honor was conferred on him two years later by the Assembly. In his book, Afrifa wrote that Nkrumah tore the 1957 constitution "into shreds" and then imposed the new one (1960) on the country to enhance his personal ambition: "the president and his lieutenants, under the guise of ensuring political calm, worked to consolidate his own future. The head of State, armed with all his powers, dismissed members of the Armed Forces and the Judiciary, when and how he liked, every time he suspected a threat to his position, or throne."[4]

On October 30, 1961, the Ghanaian Parliament passed a bill, demanded by Nkrumah, which empowered the president to establish special non-jury courts. The courts were to be made of three presidentially appointed judges whose majority decision would be sufficient to order death sentences for political opponents.[5] Nkrumah dismissed Sir Arku Korsah as Chief Justice on December 11, 1963. Korsah was the president of the special court which acquitted three prominent Ghanaians charged with treason on December 9, 1963. They were Tawiah Adamafio, former Minister of Information; Ako Adjei, former Foreign Minister; and Cofie Crabbe, former Party Executive Secretary. The charges were of conspiracy and treason.[6] Individual liberty was threatened. Even when a judge acquitted a person, the acquitted person was still held in custody. The judiciary branch was, therefore, not independent and was at the mercy of President Nkrumah.

Moreover, according to the leaders of the coup, Nkrumah meddled too much in the affairs of the military. In August, 1965, Major-General Otu, the then Chief of Defense staff and his Deputy, Major-General Ankrah, were forced by Nkrumah to retire. Afrifa stated that even though the retirement age is 55 in Ghana, both Major-General Otu and Major-General Ankrah (each of whom was 50 years old) were forced to retire because they criticized the CPP's program of indoctrinating the army with the ideology of Nkrumaism. And, according to Afrifa, membership forms were sent to the military to complete. Even though most of them refused to complete the CPP party membership forms, some officers were forced to join the CPP. Afrifa, like the majority of the army, believed that the army must be above party politics.[7]

Nkrumah's Inability to Abolish Social Inequalities

Before independence, the British officials in Ghana were leading affluent lives while the Ghanaians were living in poverty. When the CPP game into power, the Ghanaians anticipated that this kind of inequality would no longer exist as Nkrumah's socialism presupposed. On the contrary, CPP officials enjoyed nice homes, drove expensive cars, and lived, in fact, more affluently than the former British officials. Colonel Afrifa observed that:

> Nkrumah's new class promised to abolish social differences, but ... in reality it acted exactly in the opposite direction. Nkrumah's new class led a life of opulence and extravagance in contrast to the growing misery to which the rest of the country was being subjected.[8]

Thus, poor Ghanaians continued to live in slums. It must also be said that even though Nkrumah had constructed the magnificent Volta Dam, the electricity did not reach the majority of the people, especially the villagers.

Wasting of Resources

In an effort to maintain his popularity, Nkrumah embarked upon massive infrastructure programs, an example of which was the Akosombo Dam.

The military and the opposition parties accused Nkrumah of bringing Ghana to the brink of total bankruptcy. The Akosombo Dam cost the country $157 million; he also built a $12 million aluminium plant in Tema to make use of the hydroelectric power generated by the dam. All these projects were considered wasteful by the military and the opposition parties, since it was going to cost over one billion dollars if Akosombo Dam power was going to be used to supply power to the needed areas.[9]

The Volta Dam project was not a wasteful one. Ghanaians have come to realize that the Volta Dam project was a major economic achievement of Nkrumah's rule. It has made Ghana one of the few developing countries with more electricity than it could use. People criticized Nkrumah because the project did not give a direct benefit to those in the rural areas who formed the majority of Ghana's population. The question that may be difficult to answer is whether or not Ghana really needed the project at the time Nkrumah constructed it. Even with the construction of the dam, Ghana continued to be an agrarian country with cocoa as the main crop, which means that the dam was not able to build Ghana into a modern industrial society.

The military and the opposition parties accused Nkrumah of wasting money to build statues. Ghana's 1964 spending projections had included a $560,000 budget item for statues and monuments of Nkrumah.[10] This shows Nkrumah's belief in political symbolism. As the theory says, a charismatic leader adopts a strategy of making portraits of himself to be displayed at public arenas as a way of communicating his role to the people and Nkrumah tried to do this. Nkrumah's picture appeared on coins and stamps. Schools, public buildings, and state farms were named after him.[11]

Despite the scant resources available, Nkrumah diverted some of these resources to establish his own private army, the President's Own Guard Regiment (POGR), in 1963, following two bomb assassination attempts on his life, one on August 1, 1962, while he was being driven through Kulungugu in northern Ghana; and the other on September 9, 1963, near the Flagstaff House, his residence.[12] After these assassination attempts, Nkrumah began to question the loyalty of the army and police, and so he established his own army. The military and the police were displeased as

Nkrumah made efforts to weaken the regular army and the police by cutting their expenditures. For example, the regular army's fringe benefits such as rent, water, and telephone allowances were cut. The regular army accused Nkrumah of misdirecting the nation's scant resources to develop his own private forces instead of the nation's army.[13] The regular army was threatened by the POGR which was favorably treated and had all the fringe benefits the regular army used to enjoy. Colonel Afrifa described the mood of the regular army in 1965:

> Our clothes are virtually in tatters. We had no ammunition. The burden of taxation was heavy. The cost of living for the ordinary soldier was high. The army was virtually at the hands of politicians who treated it with arrogance and even open contempt. We are also aware that the President's Own Guard Regiment were receiving kingly treatment. Their pay was higher and it was an open fact that they possess better equipment. The men who had been transferred (to the POGR) from the Regular Army no longer owed any allegiance and loyalty to the Chief of Defence Staff, but to Kwame Nkrumah who had become their commanding officer.[14]

The military and police blamed Nkrumah as a selfish element who was concerned with his own security, but not the security of the entire nation. It is in this atmosphere of apprehension that fleeting thoughts of ousting Nkrumah began to take concrete form in the minds of the army and police officials.

Corruption

The military accused Nkrumah's regime of being corrupt. CPP politicians were criticized for amassing fortunes from kickbacks on government contracts with foreign contractors. Nkrumah's own fortune gained in this manner was estimated at $98 million.[15] These charges are not necessarily correct. Because the system did not allow for opposition or criticism, the CPP government was able to protect these malpractices. The single-party regime was an instrument of coercion which the CPP officials used to further their personal interests. The public became discontented and was ready to support a new regime; hence, the public readily supported the coup d'état. One might argue that it was, of course, the Ghanaian masses who paid for the cost of the corrupt relationships between foreign firms and the venal CPP politicians.

Cultural factors were primarily responsible for corruption in Ghana. Persistence of traditional values is the main cause of the problem. For example, the emphasis in African culture is achievement through clan cooperation rather than through self-help. Therefore, neglecting one's family is the most terrible thing one can do. So when one member of the extended family is in office, he tries to grant favors to relatives and friends. Moreover, everybody takes part in the corrupt practices, not just Nkrumah and the CPP politicians. Ghanaians do not look at the practice of giving a gift which usually takes the form of money as corruptive, but rather accept it as a way of life. Foreign observers looked at the problem as one of corruption without understanding the context within which it was occurring. Also, the fact that there was persistence of corruption long after the demise of the CPP indicates that the problem lies deeper than in the one-party system.

One should not lose sight of the fact that Nkrumah lacked the capital necessary for him to play a progressive role in directing the modernization of Ghana. Aside from the fact that Ghana did not have enough money to finance the socialist programs, Nkrumah had to depend on inexperienced elites. When Nkrumah made the effort to improve the school system, the richer people paid money and gave other gifts to school officials to reserve the best schools for their children.[16] This really negated Nkrumah's effort to train the children, because children who might have succeeded were denied admission to those well-equipped schools because they came from poor families.

Economic Problems

The general expectation of the people before independence was that after independence economic progress would occur, but it failed to materialize at the speed they expected.

The demand among Nkrumah's followers for the immediate achievement of the party's promised goal was perhaps the greatest strain on the retention of his political popularity. Table 5 illustrates the kinds of programs the people expected the CPP to embark upon.[17]

When asked what the Ghanaians expected of their government, desire for guaranteed jobs, reduction in the cost of living, and the provision of housing, better roads, more health clinics, and more food seemed to be of great significance. These programs proved to be ineffective. For example, housing was constrained by the high cost of imported materials. Failure in the health field was attributed to lack of effective and efficient health management and administrative services, and also inequitable distribution of health services. Also, when asked what issues the CPP government should act upon quickly, the majority of the masses chose economic matters most often. Next in order of importance were housing, transportation, and aid to the rural areas.

Table 5
Ghanaians' Expectations of the CPP Government

	Activity	Number	Percent
1.	Guarantee employment and reduce the cost of living	27	23.7
2.	Provide housing	30	17.5
3.	Provide better roads	16	14.0
4.	Provide free education	14	12.3
5.	Provide more and better food	7	6.1
6.	Provide more health clinics	6	5.3
7.	Guarantee political freedoms	5	4.4
8.	Better communications system	5	4.4
9.	Provide piped water	3	2.6
10.	Other[a]	11	9.6
	Total	124	100.0

[a] Personal expectations (e.g., "increase my salary").

Source: James A. McCain, "Attitudes Towards Socialism, Policy, and Leadership in Ghana," *African Studies Review,* 11 (1979), p. 163. A survey was conducted in which 124 Ghanaians, comprising of elites and Ghanaian masses, were the subjects of this survey. (See footnote 17.)

Economic dissatisfaction erupted into strikes between 1958 and 1962. Thousands of Ghanaian workers went on strike to protest against a government austerity program and increase in the price of basic commodities like soap, flour, sugar, and other staples. Scarcity of these products has been a problem to this day, which means that the problem of scarcity is the problem of the entire nation, the cause of which had nothing to do with

Nkrumah as a leader. Ghana is an agrarian country; she has to import these essential food products. Because of the lack of foreign exchange, which is reflective of her poor resource base, it makes it almost impossible for the government to meet its financial obligations, especially when it requires foreign exchange.

From the late 1950s onwards, the price of Ghana's main export, cocoa, was a victim of the world market.[18] The income which Ghana derived from cocoa depended primarily not on the amount of cocoa produced, but on the price which powerful world forces determined. In 1962, the price of cocoa was $698.25 per long ton. By 1964, the price fell to $245 per long ton.[19] And since cocoa repesented over 60 percent of the total value of Ghanaian export, it brought about a series of balance of payments deficits. In 1961, there was a deficit of $67.6 million and $62.6 million in 1963.[20]

Nkrumah's government was unable to initiate an international agreement on cocoa as new nations, like Ghana, are dependent on international markets. International Cocoa Agreements were made during International Cocoa Conferences to prevent excessive cocoa price fluctuations. The dilemma was that there were differences between producers and consumers over export quotas and buffer stock transactions.[21]

Government-employed railroad workers struck. The workers' chief grievances stemmed from financial and economic measures taken by the CPP government, especially the imposition of income taxes, a freeze on salary increases, and a compulsory saving scheme under which 5 percent of all wages and salaries and 10 percent of all other earnings were to be used to purchase a Ten-Year National Development bond, earning 2 percent tax-free interest. Nkrumah also put high taxes on beer, liquor, tobacco, diesel oil, sugar, flour, and other foods.[22] All these incurred the displeasure of the Ghanaians. But if development was to come about, money had to be generated from somewhere. The problem was that Ghanaians saw no benefits from sacrifice.

Conflict with the Chiefs

Another group of dissatisfied people was the chiefs whose traditional role had been curtailed by the CPP government.[23] This is in contrast to the charismatic theory. For Nkrumah to consolidate his appeal, he should have preserved the traditional institutions, because his charismatic legitimacy was to some extent to be based on or tied to tradition.

Another problem one may anticipate was that, in any society where rational-legal authority is replacing traditional, there is conflict in deciding what cases should be decided by which institution. The courts in Ghana had some difficulty in obtaining satisfactory evidence as to what was native custom. The basic problem Nkrumah faced in his dealings with the chiefs was that the chiefs stubbornly insisted on the preservation of the old customs.

External Problems

Nkrumah's foreign policy created problems for him.

His Communist Ties and Reliance on Foreign Aid

Nkrumah was accused of being biased towards communism which tended to contradict his neutrality and non-alignment policy. Nkrumah had very close ties with the Soviet Union and Communist China. The United States wanted Ghana to lean towards the West.[24] About 1,000 Russians had been assigned to Ghanaian schools and aid projects. Moscow also had committed $90 million in loans and technical aid. Communist China's $42 million aid was largely in the planning stage. The U.S. and all European countries pledged a total of only $80 million to Ghana in aid.[25] After the coup, Ghana's new ruling body, the National Liberation Council (NLC), ordered the expulsion of the Soviets for fear that the Soviets might plan a countercoup.

Foreign firms in Ghana were asked by Nkrumah to extend substantial credit to the Ghana government. The finances of Ghana were shaky and Nkrumah was reluctantly compelled to resort to heavy dependence on foreign aid.

Ghana's financial position had been precarious for a long time. According to the 1963 Economic Survey, the balance of payments deficit grew from $68.6 million in 1962 to $112.7 million in 1963 with reserves dropping from $183.7 million in 1962 to $117.6 million in 1963.[26] Caught in this labyrinth of financial catastrophe, it was probably the right move for Nkrumah to request foreign commercial firms to tide him over the existing shortage of foreign exchange. To the educated elite and the mass public, this move contradicted Nkrumah's policy of anti-imperialism. Nkrumah had earlier castigated neocolonialism, but when he became frustrated over the financial situation in Ghana, he contravened the very doctrine he had previously supported, a circumstance which incurred great public outcry.[27]

Pan-Africanism

Other critics observed that Nkrumah devoted too much time to international matters and did very little to improve conditions at home.[28] As discussed elsewhere, Nkrumah believed that the independence of Ghana was meaningless if other African states were still under colonial rule. Although this statement contains very strong pan-Africanist feelings, the difficulty lies in how Nkrumah was going to approach this problem of African liberation.

Nkrumah identified and somewhat effectively proclaimed himself as the leader of pan-Africanism. Nkrumah could have done this in Ghana, but on the international scene, it proved to be a very hard task. The formation of the Continental Union Government of Africa with Nkrumah as the first president failed because other African countries saw it to be a threat and also in violation of Article 3 of the OAU Charter, which calls for member states to respect other member countries' sovereignty and should, therefore, abide by the clause of "non-interference" in their internal affairs.[29] This implies that charisma is not international or worldwide. Charisma in one country may be labeled as dictatorship or autocracy in the other as the theory says. No wonder, Nkrumah's charisma could not transfer to other African states.

The internal problems coupled with external ones made the February 24, 1966, coup almost inevitable. While Nkrumah was traveling from Rangoon, Burma to Peking on his way to Hanoi for a Vietnam peace mission, he was overthrown in Ghana by the military.[30] He sought asylum in Guinea and died of cancer on April 27, 1972, in Rumania, and his body was thereupon returned to Ghana for state burial in his hometown of Nkroful.[31]

The overthrow of Nkrumah demonstrates that the masses, army, and civil servants, all of whom supported the coup, realized that the bargains struck by Nkrumah and other political elites, were worthless to them. Ghanaians expected achievements in satisfaction of the huge promises Nkrumah made. But, because of limited resources, maladministration, and other factors, and also Nkrumah's divided attention, some of his goals were not achieved. Probably if he had geared all his efforts towards freedom and economic development of Ghana, it would have been better. All the same, it can be asserted that the coup was not avoidable as by 1966, Nkrumah's charisma had eroded.

Probably Nkrumah did not realize that political popularity in voluntaristic environment is based on mass support, which can easily turn into mass opposition. Nkrumah tried to avoid his confrontation with the people. Although it is true that his charisma gained him massive political support, he failed to address the problem when it began to decline. Instead of dealing with the problems, he resorted to repression which became increasingly oppressive at home and abroad. Even though Nkrumah may not deserve all the blame, he had some of it. For example, while it is justified to blame Nkrumah for flagrant violations of civil rights and liberties, it is not justified to blame him for lack of resources. Even though politically wise, it was economically unjustified for Nkrumah to spend $100 million to construct a convention center for the OAU meeting.

Quite unfortunately, the military and his political opponents seemed to blame him for all the problems which are very common in transitional states. The Ghanaians had high expectations, but because Nkrumah did not have sufficient resources to meet these needs, he lost favor in the eyes of the public. Perhaps, if he had promised fewer projects and accomplished more, he might have maintained for a longer period of time the solid support he had at the beginning of his regime.

Endnotes

1 James V. Downton, *Rebel Leadership* (New York: The Free Press, 1973), p. 215.

2 Colonel A.A. Afrifa, *The Ghana Coup: 24th February 1966* (London: Frank Cass and Company Limited, 1967), p. 85.

3 Thomas A. Howell and Jeffrey P. Rajasooria, *Ghana and Nkrumah* (New York: Facts on File, Inc., 1972), p. 114.

4 Afrifa, *The Ghana Coup: 24th February 1966*, p. 63.

5 Howell and Rajasooria, *Ghana and Nkrumah*, p. 75.

6 Ibid., p. 85.

[7] Afrifa, *The Ghana Coup: 24th February 1966,* p. 99.

[8] Ibid., pp. 84-85.

[9] Howell and Rajasooria, *Ghana and Nkrumah,* pp. 112, 114,

[10] Ibid.

[11] David Apter, "Ghana," in *Political Parties and National Integration in Tropical Africa,* eds. James S. Coleman and Carl G. Rosberg (Berkeley: University of California Press, 1964), p. 304; and Ann Ruth Willner, *Charismatic Political Leadership* (Princeton: Princeton University Press, 1968), pp. 101-102.

[12] Howell and Rajasooria, *Ghana and Nkrumah,* p. 114; also Ernest W. Lefever, *Spear and Scepter: Army, Police and Politics in Tropical Africa* (Washington, D.C.: The Brookings Institution, 1970), pp. 45, 53.

[13] Ibid.

[14] Afrifa, *The Ghana Coup: 24th February 1966,* pp. 99-100, 103.

[15] Martin Kilson, "African Autocracy," *Africa Today* (April 1966), pp. 4-6.

[16] Ibid., p. 6.

[17] James A. McCain, "Attitudes Towards Socialism, Policy and Leadership in Ghana," *African Studies Review,* 22 (1979), p.163. The survey was conducted in 1974-1975 by the University of Ghana, Legon. The sample was randomly drawn from the Ghanaian elites (corporate executives, and middle-level bureaucrats and the like) and also drawn from the Ghanaian masses (composed of sales clerks, cooks, secretaries, factory workers, and the like).

[18] Kwame Nkrumah, *Revolutionary Path* (London: Panaf, 1973), p. 376.

[19] Roger Genoud, *Nationalism and Economic Development in Ghana* (New York: Praeger Publishers, 1969), p. 98.

[20] Ibid., pp. 98-99.

[21] Shamsher Singh, Jos De Vries, et al., *Coffee Tea and Cocoa: Market Prospects and Development Lending* (Baltimore: The Johns Hopkins University Press, 1977), p. 103; Josephine F. Milburn, *British Business and Ghanaian Independence* (Hanover: The University of New England Press, 1977), pp. 113-114.

[22] Howell and Rajasooria, *Ghana and Nkrumah,* p. 73.

[23] Ibid., p. 40; also Claude Ake, "Charismatic Legitimization and Political Leadership," *Comparative Studies in Society and History,* 9 (1966), p. 9.

[24] Homer A. Jack, "Russia and the West, Cairo vs. Accra: Ideological Conflict," *Africa Today*, 6 (1959), pp. 11-12.

[25] Howell and Rajasooria, *Ghana and Nkrumah*, pp. 115-116.

[26] "Ghana," *African Institute Bulletin* (December 1964), pp. 335-336. The discrepancy of figures in footnotes 20 and 26 is due to the different sources of information.

[27] Lefever, *Spear and Scepter: Army, Police and Politics in Tropical Africa*, pp. 45, 68-71.

[28] Max Addo, *Ghana's Foreign Policy* (Accra: Waterville Publishing House, 1966), p. 31.

[29] Ibid., p. 12.

[30] Howell and Rajasooria, *Ghana and Nkrumah*, p. 113.

[31] Ibid., pp. 121, 128.

Discussion Questions

1. What caused Nkrumah's political downfall? Are the reasons compelling?

2. Why were the traditional chiefs dissatisfied with the Convention Peoples Party government?

Chapter 7
Summary and Conclusion

This study explored Nkrumah's development ideology and also the development of Ghana between 1957 and 1966. After leading Ghana to independence on March 6, 1957, he embarked upon programs which were designed to improve the standard of living of Ghanaians. Through these programs, Nkrumah enhanced his own political power by centralizing all economic and political activities with the CPP playing a dominant role.

The chapter is divided into three major sections. The first section will be devoted to a discussion of Nkrumah as a political theorist. Secondly, we will analyze Nkrumah the policy-maker. The last section will present an overall summary appraisal of Nkrumah's significance generally, and for Africa in particular.

Nkrumah, the Political Theorist

Nkrumah's concept of "consciencism" was a vital principle of his political thought.

Nkrumah's consciencism asserted that for poor countries to develop they necessarily have to firstly become politically independent, and after that to break from the world capitalist system. Thus, his consciencism presupposed the primacy of politics as a pre-condition for economic, social, and cultural development.

Nkrumah also made it clear in his "consciencism" that third-world countries should be alert to possible economic domination of their economy by outsiders even after they have gained political independence. He referred to this condition as neocolonialism.

Nkrumah's notion "consciencism" suggested that socialism should be the path towards development. Specifically, Nkrumah's socialism required the state to own the means of production and distribution of goods and services. Also, his socialism rejected private capital as the major producer of goods.

Nkrumah and other African socialists rejected the Soviet scholars' view that socialism was a rigid, universal concept. Nkrumah's socialism was more flexible which gave more scope to pragmatic application. While Potekhin and other Soviet scholars viewed capitalism as a necessary stage a country will have to pass through in order to reach socialism, Nkrumah referred to the traditional African communalism to buttress the argument that Africa could bypass the capitalist stage. What Nkrumah and other African socialists had in common was that African socialism was somehow distinctively African, rooted in African traditions, and therefore loosely identified with socialism elsewhere. This immediately made Nkrumah a distinct pragmatic practitioner of Marxism.

Nkrumah's tendency to view traditional African society as classless strongly goes against the grain of authentic Marxist thought and, in an important respect, marks Nkrumah as a syncretic theorist. Essentially, he was arguing for a change in culture, which was a rather "idealistic," not materialistic approach to social change. In other words, Nkrumah was not contented to wait until capitalist development transforms society and provoked the final class struggle. Instead, he was arguing for a social revolution, not just an economic one. Moreover, his cultural referents were traditional, indigenous, and that was something way out of line with Marxist theory, which is universalist and unsympathetic with traditional cultural values (always remember Marxism is a secular and universalist theory). But from our perspective, this is an asset, because it provides us a way of discussing Nkrumah as a unique social theorist syncretically adapting Marxism to Ghana. Nkrumah combined Marxism and nationalism, emphasizing Ghanaian and African traditions as part of its valuable national heritage.

Another fundamental principle of Nkrumah's political thought was his concept of neocolonialism. By neocolonialism, Nkrumah expressed the idea that when third-world countries gain political independence, they continue to economically depend on other countries. This concept is an enduring legacy as African and other third-world countries who have gained political independence have become victims of neocolonialism.

Nkrumah was a dedicated protagonist of the one-party state. Implicit in his theory of the single-party state was the belief that the people all have a common set of interests which could be best expressed by one one-party and one group of leaders. Nkrumah calls such a system "a people's parliamentary democracy." This legacy has become a common pattern in the newly independent states and the one which the people of Ghana demonstratively have accepted.

As a political theorist, Nkrumah had left an enduring legacy for Ghana and Africa in general. His consciencism, socialism, and neocolonialism have all contributed immensely to African political thought.

Many African countries are now independent, and are all pursuing development. Their common development strategy is socialism. Even though none of those countries has been able to avoid neocolonialism (because they cannot provide capital on their own), they are more aware that they are being exploited. They are not always silent about foreign exploitation. A common response has been the nationalization of foreign firms. However, many countries do not nationalize foreign industries as that act hurts their position of attracting other foreign investors.

What I find significant about Nkrumah as a political theorist is that he was ahead of his time. For instance, he emphasized neocolonialism in the 1950s. Inherent in this concept is the notion of dependency. It took nearly a decade before the dependency theorists took on the notion of possible exploitation of poor countries by advanced countries. Thus Nkrumah was a precursor of the dependency perspective. Moreover, as a political leader, Nkrumah was pragmatic. Even though he had knowledge of Eastern and Western political thought which he respected, he applied those ideas as they suited the Ghanaian conditions.

During the period of his leadership, he was one of a few African leaders who enjoyed international recognition.

Nkrumah as a Policy-Maker

A major area of success of Nkrumah's development programs is found in education. Nkrumah encouraged education in Ghana by making it free of charge. The fact that by the time he was overthrown (1966), Ghana had the highest enrollment rates in Africa (with the exception of South Africa) signifies success in his educational program. (This does not mean that there was open access. Rich people bought their way.) For Ghana to develop, it is necessary to have qualified Ghanaians to handle the complexities of development. For example, trained personnel in engineering and medicine would be particularly essential.

As a result of Nkrumah's stress of education, Ghana has produced more scholars than it could absorb. This is evident in the large number of Ghanaian professionals who are working in neighboring African countries.

In the area of agriculture, Nkrumah was, on the one hand, successful, and on the other hand, a failure. In terms of agricultural productivity, Nkrumah performed well as cocoa production increased during his era. In spite of the increase in cocoa productivity, Nkrumah did not have sufficient funds for his programs. As discussed earlier, he became a victim of world market forces, especially in the late 1950s and early 1960s when the world price of cocoa dropped.

Even though Nkrumah had earlier condemned exploitation, he ended up exploiting the farmers by paying them less for their produce and also by forcing them to contribute twice as much (compared to workers in non-agricultural sectors) towards his compulsory savings program. While the workers in non-agricultural sectors were able to recover their contributions when the compulsory savings program ended in 1963, the farmers lost their contributions to the government.

Even though agricultural production went up, Nkrumah's state farms failed because they were unpopular with the peasants and mismanaged by the state farms officials who kept the produce for themselves and were not made accountable for it. The CPP protected them from public criticism.

Credit is due Nkrumah for engaging in the building of the Volta River Project (VRP), the largest man-made lake in the world. Not only did the VRP provide power for industrialization, it also improved agriculture, lake transportation, employment and fisheries. There were some who blamed Nkrumah for spending too much money on the VRP and argued that the money should have been spent on other programs. Others also criticized Nkrumah for not paying attention to the resettlement problems created by the building of the VRP. I believe that it was a wise move for Nkrumah to build the VRP as Ghanaian industries today have power available to them. Also, currently, the VRP is the only significant industrialization project the Ghanaians consider as Nkrumah's major industrial achievement.

While the VRP attracted foreign investment, the case can be made that it is more profitable for capitalists to invest in other industrialized countries than to invest in third-world countries. Industrialized countries already have developed an infrastructural base and so capitalist investors need not provide one. Another reason why capitalists find the investment in industrialized countries more attractive than to invest in third-world countries is that the former tend to be more stable politically. Since only a small number of capitalists are willing to channel their investments into third-world countries, third-world countries have to compete for foreign investment. This is likely to produce unfavorable terms for the poor countries when it comes to bargaining for foreign investment.

Third-world leaders who have applied in various degrees the socialist ideology have come to the same results of near economic disaster and political instability. The almost comparable pattern of failure for the emerging African countries proposes that we should track the causes to the common uncertainties of the main development strategy which they applied, socialism itself, be it African socialism or scientific socialism. The question which is difficult to answer is: How can a country make socialism work? A number of African leaders have abandoned socialism in the latter part of the 1980s in recognition that the development of the private sector is useful. African leaders are not ready for socailsm because they do not have resources to implement it. Moreover, the implementation of socialism requires accurate data for planning, which is unavailable. During the time of Nkrumah, Nkrumah's own top-ranked government officials misappropriated public funds, and also engaged in all kinds of corruptive practices. Instead of punishing the CPP officials, the CPP protected those officials, as an attack against a CPP official was an attack against the entire CPP machinery and the nation in general. Thus Nkrumah's socialism did not yield the expected results because his socialism centralized power in the CPP which in turn protected those who abused their respective positions.

Summary Appraisal of Nkrumah's Significance

Nkrumah left an enduring legacy which still stirs the imagination. He is considered a leading figure in decolonization, state-building, nation-building, and the fight against neocolonialism by many Africans today. His programs were to nurture a national consciousness and to construct the basis for industrialization. Nkrumah had the ability to inspire Ghanaians, and indeed all Africans with a vision of future greatness of the continent, and to fill them with pride in their Africaness.

His celebrated work in neocolonialism is equally enduring. He wrote that political independence will not necessarily guarantee economic independence. Many more African countries gaining independence after Ghana's have been experiencing this condition of neocolonization as Nkrumah predicted.

Nkrumah's socialist ideology has served as a common language or system of communication for the radical spokesmen of Ghana and Africa generally. Moreover, Nkrumaism did have a significant impact on Ghana and on Africa. In the early years before independence and immediately thereafter, Nkrumaism provided the rallying phrases that stirred Africa's leaders and politically alert elites.

Nkrumah is a precursor of the dependency perspective which became popular nearly a decade after Nkrumah had stressed the possibility of unequal relationship between rich and poor countries within the international forum.

For Dr. Limann, a northerner, to have been elected president of Ghana in 1979 is an undoubted proof that Nkrumah's detribalization program had begun to show results. This does not in any way undercut the fact that the challenge of state-building and nation-building in Ghana after formal independence unleashed dangerous ethnic antagonisms. These antagonisms, combined with the drive of ruling groups to build strong states capable of standing on their own, helped to produce an authoritarian solution which seems virtually unavoidable in most third-world countries. The Ghanaian experience under Nkrumah can be taken as reasonably representative of the forces making for corrupt and authoritarian rule in Africa. In this respect, the political life of Nkrumah is instructive.

It can be deduced from this study that charismatic appeal is a locational phenomenon, not an international one. Even though Nkrumah was respected by other African countries, he was not perceived to be charismatic. The problems he faced with his Pan-Africanist program supports this claim. In addition, the theory of charismatic leadership leads us to a considerable confusion because it fails to clearly specify the place of charisma in pursuit of leader-follower relations. Concomitantly, the concept seems vague because of its failure to emphasize the fact that party popularity could inhibit the degree of personal charismatic authority. There needs to be improvement of the difference between institutional charisma which focuses on power and inspirational charisma which relieves society of its existing exigency. It seems Nkrumah fits both as the research on charismatic leadership has not really brought out such difference.

From this research, we have learned several things about development. There is no single route towards development. Third-world countries tend to pursue development via socialism. The fact that those third-world countries that have pursued the socialist development path are still not developed and have confronted the same results of near economic collapse and political instability suggests that we should investigate the general etiology of the main development strategy which they have applied, socialism itself.

Finally, it must be realized that problems in transitional societies are many. They cannot be solved overnight because these countries lack the ingredients needed–lack of resources, inadequately trained and experienced elites, and also disunity which is quite manifested in tribalism. Although Nkrumah was overthrown, he must be credited as being a pacesetter of African development who is remembered up to this day in Ghana, Africa, and the rest of the world.

Discussion Questions

1. How distinctive was Nkrumah as a political theorist?

2. Present a critical appraisal of Nkrumah's significance in world politics.

Bibliography

Books

Addo, Max. *Ghana's Foreign Policy*. Accra: Waterville Publishing House, 1966.

Afrifa, Colonel A.A. *The Ghana Coup: 24th February 1966*. London: Frank Cass and Company Limited, 1967.

Afriyie, E.K. Report on the Preliminary Social Survey of Foue Krachi Area "G.E." Villages. *Volta Lake Reserach Project, May 1969*.

Allen, C. and Johnson, R.W. *African Perspectives: Papers in the History, Politics and Economics of Africa*. London: Cambridge University Press, 1970.

Alexander, Robert J. *Prophets of the Revolution*. New York: Macmillan Company, 1962.

Amnesty International Report: 1979, London: International Publications, 1979.

Amnesty International Report: 1982. London: International Publications, 1982.

Amonoo, Ben., *Ghana 1957-1966: The Politics of Institutional Dualism*. London: George Allen and Unwin, 1981.

Apter, David E."Ghana." In *Political Parties and National Integration in Tropical Africa*. Edited by James S. Coleman and Carl G. Rosberg. Berkeley: University of California Press, 1964.

Apter, David E. *Ghana in Transition*. New York: Atheneum, 1963.

Apter, David E. *The Politics of Modernization*. Chicago: The University of Chicago Press, 1965.

Austin, Dennis. *Politics in Ghana, 1946-1960*. London: Oxford University Press, 1970.

Background to Agricultural Policy. Faculty of Agriculture: University of Ghana, April 1969.

Bendix, Reinhard. *Max Weber: An Intellectual Portrait*. London: Methuen, 1966.

Bird, John. *Report on Volta River Scheme*. Accra: West African Aluminum Limited, 1949.

Birmingham, W.B., Neustadt, I., and Omaboe, E.N. *A Study of Contemporary Ghana: The Economy of Ghana,* I. Evanston: Northwestern University Press, 1966.

Bretton, H. *The Rise and Fall of Kwame Nkrumah.* London: Pall Mall, 1967.

Callaway, Barbara and Card, Emily. "Political Constraints on Economic Development in Ghana." In *The State of the Nations: Constraints on Development in Independent Africa.* Edited by Michael F. Lofchie. Berkeley: University of California Press, 1971.

Cardoso, Fernando Henriqué. *Dependency and Development.* Translated by Marjory Mattingly Urquidi. Berkeley: University of California Press, 1979.

Casanova, Pablo Gonzalez. *Democracy in Mexico.* Translated by Danielle Salti. New York: Oxford University Press, 1970.

Cefkin, J. Leo *The Background of Current World Problems.,* New York: David McKay Company, Inc., 1967.

Chambers, Robert. *The Volta Resettlement Experience.* London: Pall Mall Press, 1970.

Chilcote, Ronald H. *Theories of Comparative Politics: The Search for a Paradigm.* Boulder: Westview Press, 1981.

Chilcote, Ronald H. *Theories of Development and Underdevelopment.* Boulder: Westview Press,1984.

Crowder, Michael. *West Africa under Colonial Rule.* Evanston: Northwestern University Press, 1968.

Davidson, Basil. *Black Star: A View of the Life and Times of Nkrumah.* Londn: Clark and Brendon, Ltd., 1973.

De Graft Johnson, J.C. *Background to the Volta River Project.* Kumasi: Abura Printing Press, 1955.

Dei-Anang, Michael. *The Administration of Ghana's Foreign Relations, 1957-1965.* London: The Althone Press, 1975.

Denyoh, F.M.K. "Fisheries of the Volta Lakes." In *Man-made Lakes: Their Problems and Environmental Effects.* Edited by W.C.Ackermann, G.F. White, and E.B. Worthington. Knoxville, Tenn.: International Symposium on Man-made Lakes, May 3-7, 1971.

Desfosses, Helen and Levesque, Jacques. *Sociailsm in the Third World.* New York: Praeger Publishers, 1975.

Downton, James V. *Rebel Leadership.* New York: Free Press, 1973.

Dowse, Robert E. *Modernization in Ghana and the USSR: A Comparative Study.* New York: Humanities Press, 1969.

Dzirasa, Stephen. *Political Thought of Dr. Nkrumah.* Accra: Guinea Press, n.d.

Ewusi, Kodwo. *Economic Development Planning in Ghana.* New York: Exposition Press, 1973.

Ewusi, Kodwo. *The Distribution of Money Incomes in Ghana.* Institute of Statistical, Social and Economic Research: University of Ghana Technical Pubilcation Series, No. 14, 1971.

Furtado, Celso. *Diagnosis of the Brazilian Crisis.* Translated by Suzette Macedo. Berkeley and Los Angeles: University of California Press, 1965.

Garlick, Peter C. *African Traders and Economic Development in Ghana.* London: Clarendon Press, 1971.

Genoud, Roger. *Nationalism and Economic Development in Ghana.* New York: Praeger Publishers, 1969.

Ghana Ministry of Information, *Nkrumah's Deception of Africa.* Accra-Tema: Ministry of Information, 1967.

Grant, Andrew. *Socialism and the Middle Classes.* New York: International Publishers, Inc., 1959.

Harris, Richard. *The Political Econmy of Africa.* New York: John Wiley and Sons, 1975.

Hovet, Thomas Jr. *Africa in the United Nations.* Evanston: Northwestern University Press, 1963.

Howard, Rhoda. *Colonialism and Underdevelopment in Ghana.* New York: African Publishing Company, 1978.

Howell, Thomas A. and Rajasooria. *Ghana and Nkrumah.* New York: Facts on File, Inc., 1972.

Italiaander, R. *The Leaders of Africa.* Englewood Cliffs, N.J.: Prentice Hall, 1961.

Jackson, R.G.A. *The Volta River Project: Progress.* Unilever, No. 4, 1964.

Jones, Trevor, *Ghana's First Republic 1960-1965.* London: Methuen and Company, 1976.

Jopp, Keith. *The Story of Ghana's Volta River Project.* 1965.

Kaplan, Irving, McLaughlin, et al. *Area Handbook for Ghana.* Washington, D.C.: U.S. Government Printing Office, 1971.

Kautsky, John H. *The Political Consequences of Modernization.* New York: John Wiley and Sons, Inc., 1972.

Kay, G.B. and Hymer, Stephen. *The Political Economy of Colonialism in Ghana.* Cambridge: Cambridge University Press, 1972.

Krassowski, Andrzej. *Development and the Debt Trap: Economic Planning and External Borrowing in Ghana.* London: Overseas Development Institute, 1974.

Kwame Nkrumah. London: Panaf, 1974.

Lefever, Ernest W. *Spear and Scepter: Army, Police and Politics in Tropical Africa.* Washington, D.C.: The Brookings Institutin, 1970.

Lenin, V. I. *Imperialism: The Highest Stage of Capitalism.* New York: Internatinal Publishers, 1939.

Lindert, Peter H. and Kindleberger, Charles P. *International Economics,* Homewood, Illinois: Irwin,Inc., 1982.

Lowe-McConnel, R.H. *Man-made Lakes.* London: Institute of Biology Symposium No. 15, n.d.

Marx, Karl and Engels, Friedrich, "Manifesto of the Communist Party." In *The Communist Manifesto.* Edited by Samuel H. Beer, New York: Appleton-Century-Crofts, Inc., 1955.

Milburn, Josephine F. *British Business and Ghanaian Independence.* Hanover: The University of New England Press, 1977.

Miracle, Marvin P. and Seidman, A. *State Farms in Ghana.* Land Tenure Center: University of Wisconsin, L.T.C. No. 43 (March 1968).

Moxon, James. *Volta: Man's Greatest Lake.* New York: Praeger Publishers, 1969.

Nkrumah, Kwame. *Africa Must Unite.* New York: Praeger Publishers, 1963.

Nkrumah, Kwame. *The Autobiography of Kwame Nkrumah*. New York: Thomas Nelson and Sons, 1957.

Nkrumah, Kwame. *Axioms of Kwame Nkrumah*. London: Nelson and Sons, 1967.

Nkrumah, Kwame. *Class Struggle in Africa*. New York: International Publishers, 1970.

Nkrumah, Kwame. *Consciencism: Philosophy and Ideology for Decolonization and Development*. New York: Monthly Review Press, 1965.

Nkrumah, Kwame. *Dark Days in Ghana*. London: Panaf, 1968.

Nkrumah, Kwame. *I Speak of Freedom: A Statement of African Ideology*. New York: Praeger Publishers, 1961.

Nkrumah, Kwame. *Neocolonialism: The Last Stage of Imperialism*. London: Nelson and Sons, 1965.

Nkrumah, Kwame. "Positive Action in Africa." In *Africa Speaks*. Edited by James Duffy and Robert A. Manners. New Jersey: Princeton University Press, 1961.

Nkrumah, Kwame, *Revolutionary Path*. London: Panaf,1973.

Nkrumah, Kwame. "The Future of African Law." *Voice of Africa* (April 1962).

Nkrumah, Kwame. *Towards Colonial Freedom*. New York: International Publishers, 1973.

Offiong, Daniel A. *Imperiailsm and Dependency: Obstacles to African Development*. Wshington, D.C.: Howard University Press, 1982.

Omari, T.P. *Kwame Nkrumah: The Anatomy of an African Dictatorship*. Accra: Moxon Paperbacks, 1970.

Padmore, George. *The Gold Coast Revolution*. London: Dennis Dobson Ltd., 1963.

Parsons, Talcott. "Introduction." In *The Theory of Social and Economic Organization*. Edited by Max Weber. New York: Free Press, 1947.

Parsons, Talcott. *The Social System*. Glencoe, Ill.: Free Press, 1951.

Plano, Jack C. and Greenberg, Milton. *The American Political Dictionary*. New York: Holt, Rinehart and Winston, Inc., 1963.

Potekhin, Ivan I. "On African Socialism: A Soviet View." In *African Socialism*. Edited by William H. Friedland and Carl G. Rosberg. Stanford: Stanford University Press, 1964.

Prebisch, Raul. *Change and Development--Latin America's Great Task*. New York: Praeger Publishers, 1971.

Rhoda, Howard. *Colonialism and Underdevelopment in Ghana*. New York: Africana Publishing Company, 1978.

Roxborough, Ian. *Theories of Underdevelopment*. London: McMillan Press Ltd., 1979.

Sargent, Lyman Tower. *Contemporary Political Ideologies*. Homewood,Ill.: The Dorsey Press, 1984.

Shepherd, George W. *The Politics of African Nationalism: Challenged to American Policy*. New York: Praeger Inc., 1962.

Singh, Shamsher, Vries, Jos De, et al. *Coffee, Tea and Cocoa: Market Prospects and Development Lending*. Baltimore: The Johns Hopkins University Press, 1977.

Spiro, Herbert J. "The Primacy of Political Development" In *Africa: The Primacy of Politics*. Edited by Herbert J. Spiro. New York: Random House Inc., 1966.

Thompson, Scott. *Ghana's Foreign Policy, 1957-1966*. Princeton: Princeton University Press, 1969.

Timothy, Bankhole. *Kwame Nkrumah: His Rise to Power*. Evanston: Northwestern University Press, 1961.

Waltz, Kenneth. "Theory of International Relations." In *Handbook of Political Science* (International Politics). Edited by Fred I. Greenstein and Nelson N. Polsby, Menlo Park, Calif.; Addison-Wesley Publishing Company, 1975.

Warner, D. *Ghana and the New Africa*. London: Frederick Muller Press, 1960.

Weber, Max. *From Max Weber: Essays in Sociology*. Translated by H.H. Gerth and C. Wright Mills. New York: Oxford University Press, 1958.

Weber, Max. *The Theory of Social and Economic Organization*. New York: The Free Press, 1947

Willner, Ann Ruth. *Charismatic Political Leadership.* Princeton: Princeton University Press, 1968.

Willner, Ann Ruth and Willner, Dorothy. "The Rise and Role of Charismatic Leaders." *The Annals of the American Academy of Political and Social Science,* 358 (March 1965).

Wright, Richard. *Black Power.* New York: Harper, 1954.

Young, Crawford. *Ideology and Development in Africa.* New Haven: Yale University Press, 1982.

Periodicals

Ake, Claude. "Charismatic Legitimization and Political Leadership." *Comparative Studies in Society and History,* 9 (1966), 9-12.

Apter, David E. "Nkrumah, Charisma and the Coup." *Daedalus,* 97 (Summer 1968), 740-792.

Austin, Dennis. "Elections in an African Rural Area." *Africa,* 21 (1961), 1-18.

Berret, Anthony M. "Laws and Leaders in the New States." *Africa Today,* (1966), 12-14.

Birmingham, W.B. and Jahoda, G. "A Pre-election Survey in a Semi-literate Society." *Public Opinion Quarterly,* 19 (1955), 140-152.

Bretton, H. "Current Political Thought and Practice in Ghana" *American Political Science Review,* 52 (March 1958), 46-63.

Duncan, Patrick. "Non-Violence at Accra." *Africa Today,* 6 (1959), 30-33.

Galtung, Johan. "A Structural Theory of Imperialism." *Journal of Peace Research,* 8 (1971), 81-117.

"Ghana." *African Institute Bulletin* (December 1964), 335-336.

Ghana Today, 5 (June 1961).

Greenstreet, D.K. "The Guggisberg Ten-Year Development Plan." *The Economic Bulletin of Ghana,* 8, No. 1 (1964), 21.

Grundy, Kenneth W. "Marxism-Leninism and African Underdevelopment: The Malian Approach. *International Journal,* 17 (Summer 1962), 300-304.

Grundy, Kenneth W. "The Class Struggle in Africa: An Examination of Conflicting Theories." *The Journal of Modern African Studies,* 2, No. 3 (1964), 379-393.

Grundy, Kenneth W. "The Political Ideology of Kwame Nkrumah." *Monograph Series in World Affairs,* 5, Nos. 3 and 4. Denver: University of Denver Publication (1967-68), 66-100.

Hodgkin, Thomas. "A Note on the Language of African Nationalism." In St. Anthony's Papers No. 10. Edited by Kenneth kirkwood. *African Affairs,* 1 (1961), 22-40.

Kilson, Martin. "African Autocracy." *Africa Today* (April 1966), 4-6.

Kilson, Martin. "Authoritarian and Single-Party Tendencies in African Politics." *World Politics,* 15, No. 2 (January 1963), 262-294.

Kilson, Martin. "Nationalism and Social Classes in British West Africa." *Journal of Politics,* 20, No. 2 (May 1958), 368-387.

Lagueur, Walter Z. "Communism and Nationalism in Tropical Africa." *Foreign Affairs,* 34 (July 1961), 610-621.

Lawson, Rowena M. "An Interim Appraisal of the Volta Resettlement Scheme," *Nigerian Journal of Social and Economic Studies,* 10, No. 1 (March 1968), 95-109.

Lisk, F. "Inflation in Ghana, 1964-75: Its Effects on Employment, Incomes and Industrial Relations." *International Labor Review,* 113, No. 3 (May-June 1976), 359-375.

McCain, James A. "Attitudes Towards Socialism, Policy and Leadership in Ghana," *African Studies Review,* 22 (1979), 149-163.

Nkrumah, Kwame. "African Prospect." *Foreign Affairs,* 37 (October 1958), 45-53.

Nkrumah, Kwame. "Some Aspects of Socialism in Africa." *Pan Africa* (April 1963), 13-17.

Nkrumah, Kwame. "Speech to the Workers on May Day, 1965." *Ghana Today,* 9, No. 5 (May 1965).

Rudolph, Susanne Hoeber. "The New Courage: An Essay on Gandhi's Psychology." *World Politics,* 16 (October 1963), 98-117.

Runciman, W.G. "Charismatic Legitimacy and One-Party Rule in Ghana." *European Journal of Sociology,* 4 (1963), 148-165.

Rustow, Dankwart A. "Ataturk as Founder of a State." *Daedalus,* 97 (Summer 1968), 793-828.

Shils, Edward. "The Concentration and Dispersion of Charisma." *World Politics,* 11 (October 1958), 1-19.

Sunkel, Osvado. "Big Business and Dependencies." *Foreign Affairs,* 50 (April 1972), 517-531.

Tucker, Robert C. "The Theory of Charismatic Leadership." *Daedalus,* 97 (Summer 1968), 731-755.

Waddy, B.B. "Health Problems on Man-made Lakes." *Geographical Magazine* (April 1966), 887-897.

Wallerstein, Immanuel. "Dependence in an Interdependent World: The Limited Possibilities of Transformation within the Capitalist World Economy." *African Studies Review,* 17, No. 1 (April 1974), 1-26.

Wallerstein, Immanuel. "The Political Ideology of the PDG." *Presence Africans,* 12 (First Quarter 1962), 30-41.

"What Is African Socalism?" *African Institute Bulletin,* 3, No. 9 (Septeper 1965), 223.

Government Publications

British White Paper Cmd 8702. *The Volta River Aluminum Scheme* (November 1952).

Building a Socialist State: An Address ... to the C.P.P. Study Group, April 22, 1961. Accra: Ghana Information Services, 1961.

"Conference of Heads of State and Government, Belgrade." *Ghana* (1961).

FAO/UNDP. *Volta Lake Research, Ghana: Interim Report.* Rome, 1971.

Ghana Cocoa Marketing Board at Work (1963).

Ghana, "Conference of Heads of State and Government" (1961).

Ghana: Five Year Development Plan, Part II (January 1977).

Ghana. Legislative Assembly Reports (March 1959).

Ghana Ministry of Information. *Nkrumah's Subversion in Africa.* Accra-Tema: Ministry of Information, 1966.

Ghana: Seven Year Development Plan: Report (1963-64 to 1969-70).

Ghana: Seven Year Development Plan: Report for the Second Plan Year 1965.

Great Britain. Statutory Instruments (1957, No. 277). *The Ghana (Constitution) Order in Couhcil* (1975), paragraph 54.

House of Representatives, Committee on International Relations. *Country Reports on Human Rights Practices.* Washington, D.C.: Department of State (3 February 1978).

House of Representatives, Committee on Foregn affairs, and Senate, Committee on Foreign Relations. *Coutry Reports on Human Rights Practices for 1979.* Washington, D.C.: Department of State (4 February 1980).

IBRD. *Appraisal of the Volta River Hydroelectric Project.* Washington: World Bank, 1960.

IBRD. *Appraisal of the Volta River Hydroelectric Project.* Washington: World Bank, 1961.

IBRD. *Preliminary Appraisal of the Volta River Hydroelectric Project.* Washington: World Bank, 1957.

Interview: CF-14 London (10 November 1965).

Interview: CF-103 London (10 November 1965).

Interview: CF-106 London (10 November 1965).

Jack, Homer A. "Russia and the West, Cairo vs. Accra: Ideological Conflict. *Africa Today,* 6 (1959).

Kaiser, Henry J. and Company. *Reassessment Report on the Volta River Project for the Government of Ghana.* Oakland, Calif., 1959.

Nkrumah, Kwame. *Address to the CPP Study Group in Flagstaff House* (1961).

Nkrumah, Kwame. *Speech at the Accra Arena to Celebrate the Tenth Anniversary of the Founding of the CPP* (June 12, 1959).

Nkrumah, Kwame. "What I Mean by Positive Action." *Ghana Pamphlets,* No. 1 (1949).

Off. Jnl. Parl. Debs. (October 1963), col. 353.

Off. Jnl. Parl. Debs. (August 1965), col. 107.

Parliamentary Debates, Vol. XVI, No. 35, col. 1682 (1959).

P.R. #295/60 (5 April 1960).

P.R. #311/60 (7 April 1960).

Preparatory Commission Report, The Volta River Project, Vol. 1, No. 29 (1956).

President Eisenhower and Prime Minister Nkrumah: Joint Statement. Washington, D.C.: White House (1958).

Programme of the Convention People's Party for Work and Happiness. Accra, 1962.

Quarterly Digest Statistics. Ghana, Ministry of Information: Central Bureau of Statistics, Vol. XVI, Table 55 (1969).

The Spark: Some Essential Features of Nkrumaism. Accra: Spark Publications, 1964.

Speech to Launch the Seven Year Development Plan (March 1964).

U.N. Statistics, Vol. 14 (1962).

U.N. Statistics, Vol. 16 (1964).

U.N. Statistics, Vol. 17 (1965).

U.N. Statistics, Vol. 20 (1968).

U.N. Statistics, Vol. 21 (1969).

U.N. Statistics, Vol. 26 (1974).

U.N. Statistics, Vol. 28 (1976).

U.N. Statistics, Vol. 29 (1977).

Volta River Authority (VRA), Annual Report (1970).

Volta River Authority (VRA), Annual Report (1976).

Volta River Development Act, 1961. Government of Ghana, 1961.

Volta River Project. Report on the Mid-term Project Review Mission, DP/SF/301/GHA (10 December 1969).

Willner, Dorothy. "Community Leadership." *United Nations Series,* ST/SOA/Ser. 0/36 (1960).

World Bank, Cost-Benefit Analysis: Volta River Project (1976).

World Development Report. (1979)

Newspapers

Evening News. 22 September 1958, p. 1.

Evening News. 8 June 1959, p. 1.

Evening News. 22 June 1960, p. 2.

Evening News. 20 November 1959, p. 2.

Evening News. 11 December 1959, p. 1.

Evening News. 26 January 1960, p. 2.

Evening News. 4 February 1960, p. 2.

Evening News. 21 March 1960, p. 3.

Evening News. 23 March 1960, p. 1.

Evening News. 23 March 1960, p. 2.

Evening News. 24 September 1960, p. 3.

Interview

White, Gilbert. University of Colorado, Boulder, Colorado. Interview, 22 March 1984.

Index